Clever

LEADING
YOUR
SMARTEST,
MOST
CREATIVE
PEOPLE

Clever

ROB GOFFEE
GARETH JONES

HARVARD BUSINESS PRESS

BOSTON, MASSACHUSETTS

Library of Congress Cataloging-in-Publication Data

Goffee, Robert.
    Clever: leading your smartest, most creative people / Rob Goffee, Gareth Jones.
        p. cm.
    Includes index.
    ISBN 978-1-4221-2296-9 (hardcover : alk. paper) 1. Creative ability in
business. 2. Teams in the workplace. 3. Leadership. 4. Employee motivation.
I. Jones, Gareth, 1951 Aug. 21- II. Title.
    HD53.G638 2009
    658.4'092—dc22

Clever: Possessing skill or talent

–Shorter Oxford English Dictionary

CONTENTS

ACKNOWLEDGMENTS

Our research has been led by the idea that leadership is a relationship between leader and led. It was this that stimulated our sociological interest. This, we believe, is the nexus of how people behave in organizations, of how people understand and practice leadership.

Leader and follower. Follower and leader.

It is as bare and challenging as that. How best can we understand and maximize this relationship?

This has long been the simple focus of our interest and research. In our previous book, *Why Should Anyone Be Led By You?*, we looked at both sides of the equation. Along the way, we talked to many followers as well as leaders in a wide range of organizations, industries, and institutions.

As we talked to leaders and followers, it was clear that expectations had changed. Followers did not expect to be told what to do. They wanted leadership with respect as well as rewards. Followers want, expect, and deserve the real thing from those who lead them.

There was a similar sense of shifting perspectives among the leaders we talked to. Leaders realized that certain of their followers generated huge amounts of value for the organization. Their most valuable people were crucial to the success of the organization—and yet, at the same time, often the most difficult to lead.

So, we have been on a journey. *Clever* is the latest leg. As with any journey, we have had a great deal of help and inspiration along the way.

We would like to take this opportunity to acknowledge the contribution made by Des Dearlove and Stuart Crainer to our work over the past few years. As the relationship has developed, they have helped to shape the expression of our ideas and consistently acted as a valuable source of wisdom and practical advice.

Jeff Kehoe, our editor at HBP, has managed the delicate balance between reminding us of our schedule and being a sympathetic friend superbly. His editorial interventions have been consistently helpful. Our agent, the remarkable Helen Rees, has been our protector in the sometimes mysterious world of publishing.

We would also like to thank all of those we have tested our ideas on over the last few years. Our colleagues—Jay Conger, Estelle Bowman, Costas Markides, and Laura Tyson—have provided valuable feedback. Friends have also been gently leaned on to provide their own insights and help. Thanks especially to ′ Evaleen Jaager Roy at Electronic Arts (EA), Alison and Craig Fields, and Ping Zhen.

Our assistants Lucie Grant and Jayna Patel have offered timely and helpful administrative assistance as we completed the fieldwork and the final manuscript.

Some organizations have given us access to their own clever people. In particular, we would like to thank Arup, BSI, BTG, Cisco, Credit Suisse, Electronic Arts, Fujitsu, Google, ING, Kantar, Lion Nathan, LVMH, McLaren, Microsoft, the National Health Service (NHS), Nestlé, PricewaterhouseCoopers (PwC), Roche, Skolkova, Thermax, UBS, and the Universities of London, New South Wales, Oxford, and Western Australia.

ACKNOWLEDGMENTS

We are grateful to all of the following people, who gave their time generously:

Werner Bauer, Nestlé

Patrick Bermingham, McLaren

Lucy Bradshaw, Electronic Arts

Neil Buckley, ING

Tristram Carfrae, Arup

Jane Collins, Great Ormond Street Hospital

Louis Coutts, Coutts & Connor

Sir Graeme Davies, University of London

Mark de Simone, Cisco

Andreas Dohmen, Cisco

Peter Donnelly, Oxford University

Mary Eckenrod, Kraft

Mary Edwards, Basingstoke and North Hampshire NHS
    Foundation Trust

Alison Fields

Craig Fields

Aristides Garces, Microsoft

David Gardner, formerly of Electronic Arts

Lucy Gill, Kantar

William "Bing" Gordon, Electronic Arts

Fred Hilmer, University of New South Wales

Tracey Horton, University of Western Australia Business School

Franz Humer, Roche

Christina Kite, Cisco

Kai-Fu Lee, Google

Peter Lees, NHS Leadership Centre, National Health Service

Alain Lorenzo, LVMH

Marcus Mackay

Louise Makin, BTG plc

Alex Marin, ING

Julie McEver, New Philanthropy Capital

Vicky Medley, BSI Products

Suraj Moraje, McKinsey & Company

Rob Murray, Lion Nathan

Jonathan Neale, McLaren Racing

David Nicholson, National Health Service

Kamlesh Pande, Thermax

Glen Poor, Microsoft

Ocean Quigley, Electronic Arts

Sreekala Ramamurthy, Wipro

Pierre-Yves Roussel, LVMH

Andrzej Rusewicz, Microsoft

Marc Silvester, Fujitsu Services

Jim Singh, Nestlé

Sir Martin Sorrell, WPP

Osvaldo Spadano, Venda Technology Group

Stephen Taylor, Microsoft

Dan Teodosiu, Microsoft

Alastair Trivett, BSI Products

Laura Tyson, formerly of London Business School

Saul Van Beurden, ING

Ruben Vardanian, Moscow School of Management Skolkovo

ACKNOWLEDGMENTS

Mathieu Verougstraete, ING

Jeremy Watson, Arup

Joe Woolf, Atlas Industries

Will Wright, Electronic Arts

Carolyn Yates, Google

Finally, we would also like to thank both our families, who have tolerated the antisocial obsessions that the work has entailed. Their indulgence and support has been most welcome.

—Rob Goffee and Gareth Jones
February 2009

INTRODUCTION

Most organizations have them. They are individuals who make a disproportionate contribution to what the organization does. They habitually punch above their weight. Sometimes there are lots of them, while other times there are just a handful. Exactly who they are and what they do varies greatly according to the context.

In a *Harvard Business Review* article, we labeled such individuals "clever people." In the United States, we know, being clever carries connotations of being overly smart and difficult. But we prefer the English interpretation—being skilled and talented—with an acceptance that being smart usually comes with a few rough edges.

Who do we mean when we talk of clever people? Well, think, for example, of software programmers or pharmaceutical researchers who create a new piece of code or a new drug that can potentially bankroll the entire organization for a decade. Or think of investment bankers or tax accountants who find a tax-efficient way to structure a merger deal, or market researchers who see patterns in consumer spending that no one else can detect, and spot a new market category.

Truth be told, when we set out to learn more about these smart and powerful, yet often recalcitrant, clever people, we thought we would be talking to consultants, lawyers, investment bankers, R&D wizards, and other similar smart professionals. We did, but we also found value-creating brilliance in a huge variety of places: in schools, in hospitals, in fast moving consumer goods (FMCG) businesses, in breweries—and not just in the R&D departments. Clever people can be any of these and more: school teachers, university and hospital administrators, curators at museums. But as different as they are, they are all capable of creating huge amounts of value for their organizations.

Clever is their book and a book for those who are charged with unleashing their most remarkable potential.

CLEVER HEAD TURNING

So, the clever people who inhabit the pages that follow *are* valuable—extremely. In fact, we would argue that they are the most valuable people the organization has—more valuable than their leaders (more valuable, perhaps, even than the CEO). Or, at least, they have the potential to be more valuable than anyone else. But that does not mean that they will automatically realize that potential—far from it. And that's precisely the point: the clever people we are talking about are capable of great things, but only if the organizational and leadership context enables them to realize their potential. "My job is to make sure the organization works for you," we heard one CEO tell his staff at a company conference.

As we talked to more and more people throughout the world, it became clear that these clever people have a symbiotic relationship with their leaders and with their organizations. Indeed, this has become one of the book's central themes. We have seen organizations that are full of clevers. We have also seen organizations that are well led. But the most successful organizations of the future will have to be both. Without clever people, leaders cannot hope to succeed. Without good leadership, clevers can never realize their full potential. They are in it together. Clevers need leaders; and leaders need clevers. And both need organizations. Together, they can achieve great things. But one without the other will fail.

As we learned more about these clever people, the question facing leaders and organizations became clear: how do you corral a group of extremely smart and highly creative individuals into an organization, and then inspire them not only to achieve their fullest potential as individuals, but to do so in a way that creates wealth and value for all your stakeholders: customers, shareholders, and the wider community? How can organizations and the clever individuals who make them up harness their potential to achieve great outcomes—for all those involved?

Of course, the need to inspire people—clever or otherwise—to achieve their highest potential is nothing new. Open any book on organizations, and you will see some familiar themes: how to motivate employees, how to keep them engaged, how to build morale. In short, the problem is usually seen as how to make employees *more* valuable to the organization. This book turns that challenge on its head. *Clever* is concerned with making *organizations* more valuable to clever people.

That is a substantial challenge, and it is one that requires two realizations. First, there needs to be an appreciation that clever people have a symbiotic relationship with their organizations. They need the sociability, infrastructure, credibility, resources, and scale offered by an organization, as much as the organization needs their value-generating power.

Second, unleashing the potential of clever people demands a new style of leadership. Leaders can no longer be the sole driving force for progress. They are not the one who leads the charge up the mountain. Rather, they must identify the clever people with the potential to reach the summit, connect them with others, and help them get there. Once leadership was all about planting your flag on the summit and standing heroically for a photograph. Now the leader is the one pacing anxiously at base camp waiting to hear good news.

SHIFTING STRANDS

Our previous work drew on our sociological backgrounds. In contrast to the predominant research traditions on leadership, we believe that leadership is a *relationship* between the leaders and the led. It is as much illuminated by sociological concepts as it is by the psyche of the leader. *Clever* places even greater emphasis on the relationship between the leader and the led. Indeed, it shifts the balance dramatically. The leader is no longer automatically and exclusively in the spotlight. The dividing line between leaders and followers is increasingly fuzzy. Many of the people we encountered in our research moved from one role to the other—albeit with varying degrees of comfort. It is as if the spotlight is on the stage and there is no single person basking in its light, but a captivating drama is unfolding in the wings.

While many of the attitudes, aspirations, and approaches we look at in *Clever* appear to be fundamental challenges to long-established organizational norms, many have a reassuringly familiar ring to them. Even though the shift to the knowledge economy is a relatively recent phenomenon, many of the basic issues were formulated in classic sociological theory.

This should come as no surprise. The changes occurring in the business world run deeper than merely the relationship between the leaders and the led. They extend to all aspects of our daily lives. Many of the issues we discuss in *Clever* not only affect our working lives but have consequences for the kind of societies we will live in.

The relationship between the organization of work and the organization of society was the central obsession of Karl Marx. Marx saw the central problem for the capitalist enterprise as how to transform the purchase of labor (which is, after all, only a potential) into real work. Strangely, most modern textbooks on organization tacitly accept this proposition. The central issues are seen as motivating the workforce and securing their compliance or, in the most recent books, their commitment. It is curious that management theory shares many fundamental assumptions with management's most profound critic.[1]

So Marx and management theory have more in common than you might imagine. But the people who populate this book turn common assumptions on their head. They don't need motivating. Further, the complexity of their knowledge suggests not a deskilling of work but a radical *reskilling*: in effect, an increase in the variability of labor.

Max Weber, Marx's most serious critic, thought that the rise of the capitalist enterprise was not the most significant characteristic of the modern era. From his perspective, the growth and domination of *bureaucratic* organizations was the defining feature of the modern period. Weber believed that the bureaucratic organization was the embodiment of *technical rationality*: a logic that says whatever your problem, we can find a technical solution to it—a logic of means, not ends.[2]

Many of the people we have interviewed in the course of this research exemplify not the rationality of the bureaucracy but a *value rationality*: a logic of goals and ends. This is characteristic of organizations that have an aspirational cause.

And it's not just at evangelical organizations like Google; you will find the same passion echoed at Nestlé, BMW, Arup, Microsoft, Roche, the United Kingdom's National Health Service, schools and universities, and a whole host of organizations featured in this book. The clever organizations of the future may rest not on instrumental rationality, the stuff of microeconomic theory, but on value rationality.[3]

Weber believed that the bureaucratic organization would triumph.

The subjects of this book subvert this view. They reject the principles of bureaucratic organizations; they struggle against standardization of their work and assert the uniqueness of their contribution.

The clever people who feature in *Clever* feel and express strong needs for a workplace that generates meaning. They explicitly demand a sense of purpose, and when this is shared, clever people deliver high-performance organizations.

WHOLLY, HUMBLY HAPPY

We believe that leading clever people is one of the greatest challenges facing organizations today. It can be extraordinarily trying and often requires huge personal sacrifice and humility on the part of the leader. Happily, it is also one of the most satisfying roles a leader can perform. It is about working with the most talented individuals, people who are capable of incredible achievements. "There's a lot of clever people here. It's the adrenaline you get from working with them that I like," one leader told us.[4] We also believe passionately that those leaders who embrace the challenge and get it right have an opportunity to make an enormous contribution to their organizations—and to the world at large. And to be sure, the world faces enormous challenges—economic recession, climate change, food shortages, poverty, health care—all of which demand clever solutions.

We think and hope these are not groundlessly grandiose claims. There are no limits to what mankind can achieve. Witness the pace of change in the health-care sector, where genetic science is opening new doors at an unprecedented rate. But with that comes real danger. The business leaders of tomorrow will be held accountable not simply for financial results, but for moral outcomes as well.

In his 1978 book *Leadership*, James MacGregor Burns wrote that civilization depended on its "transforming" leaders—those who didn't just solve the problems handed to them, but who helped to raise society as a whole to higher levels of motivation and morality.[5] Other business writers picked up the theme: corporations, as Warren Bennis sagely put it, need leaders who do not just "do things right" but also "do the right thing."[6]

This will be even more important as we embrace the brave new world of the twenty-first century. It is the job of future leaders to create an environment where brilliant people can flourish. "The empires of the future will be the empires of the mind," Winston Churchill famously observed. Today, Churchill's words appear more prescient than ever.

READING *CLEVER*

Clever, we hope, provides answers to the question of how clever people should, and must, be led to maximize their potential, their personal, organizational, and societal value. Our focus throughout is on clever individuals who work within organizations.

In part 1, Leader and Led, we consider clever people as individuals. In chapter 1, we look at who these people are, their common characteristics, and why they are increasingly powerful. In chapter 2, we examine the challenges they present to leaders; in particular, we discuss what leaders can do to identify and get the best out of these clever individuals.

Yet, clever as they are, most of the individuals do not create value in isolation. In the majority of cases—whether they like it or not—they are part of a team, whose cleverness can be amplified through contact with other clevers. In part 2, we turn our attention to clever people in teams. In chapter 3, we consider the (sometimes volatile) cocktail of clever people working together. Teams of clever people, we quickly discovered, are not necessarily the same thing as clever teams. Here we describe a range of different clever teams in a variety of organizational contexts.

In chapter 4, we explore the fundamental shared tensions that arise between the nature of the work undertaken by clever teams and the social dynamics of the teams themselves. As a result of our research, we offer suggestions on how best to lead clever teams.

In part 3, Clever Organizations, we move to the organizational level. In chapter 5, we examine the contours of clever organizations. Here we examine three major organizational types and their associated challenges. Then, in chapter 6, we look forward, to consider the challenges and possible solutions for leading the clever organizations of the future.

For us, *Clever* has been a fascinating intellectual journey. We have met some incredibly interesting people in organizations all over the world who it was hard not to be excited by. We just hope that we manage to convey some of this excitement to you. More than ever, the world needs clever people and clever organizations.

PART ONE

LEADER AND LED

1 UNDERSTANDING CLEVER PEOPLE

THE FIRST AND MOST obvious point to make is that clever people are not simply those with the highest IQ or the most impressive academic qualifications (although many of them do score highly on these two measures). Our conversations and observations have led us to develop a simple definition:

> **Clever people are highly talented individuals with the potential to create disproportionate amounts of value from the resources that the organization makes available to them.**

This second point is significant. There are many highly talented individuals who are capable of producing remarkable results on their own—that is to say, outside of an organization. These stand-alone clever people include artists, solo musicians, and other free agents. But they are not the people we are talking about. We use the term *clever people* to refer specifically to talented individuals who *need* an organization to achieve their full potential.

Precisely what they do, of course, depends on the context. In pharmaceutical companies they carry out scientific research and produce ideas for new drugs; in professional services firms they solve complex client problems; in ad agencies they understand customers and brand values, and craft highly innovative communications that connect the two. But whatever they do, they do it extraordinarily.

WILL POWER

Consider Will Wright. Intensely, energetically intelligent, Wright is regarded as one of the pioneers and greatest talents in the computer-gaming world. He is the man behind the original *SimCity*, which spawned an entire series of *Sims* games allowing players to create their own simulated towns, homes, and families. Technologically, aesthetically, and commercially, *SimCity* is a place of beauty. The computer game, originally launched in 1989, is an urban planner's dream. It allows gamers to create their own 3-D cities and manage their growth and prosperity. For the city to flourish and grow, the player must manage its finances, environment, and quality of life.

SimCity is a high-tech melting pot of ideas and images, a place where the traditional dollhouse meets utopian urban planning, where every player is imbued with the all-seeing vision of Big Brother and the power of God—or, at least, the local mayor. There are no winners. There are no guns or evil enemies. There is only the player, a screen, and the power to shape imaginary families, households, and towns.

SimCity was an instant hit for California-based Maxis, a subsidiary of Electronic Arts (EA). It has generated a host of spin-offs. The *Sims* series has now sold many millions of copies. For Will Wright, fictional *Sims* opened real doors. We sat and talked in the studio he leads in San Francisco where his new project, named *Spore*, was taking shape (it was released in September 2008).[1]

As Wikipedia—in many ways the self-appointed gospel of clever—explains it, "*Spore* is a multi-genre massive single-player online metaverse video game. It allows a player to control the development of a species from its beginnings as a unicellular organism, through development as an intelligent and social creature, to interstellar exploration as a space-faring culture. It has drawn wide attention for its massive scope, and its use of open-ended gameplay and procedural generation."

It is, an executive confides, also "audaciously ambitious and expensive." *Spore* essentially switches roles so that the players are actually creating the game. In most games, the player experiences the world created by the artist; in *Spore,* players create that experience. "We've had to make systems where all these things that are normally done by professionals for nice salaries are being done by the player, so the player makes a creature and we have to work out how do you put skin on it, how do you surface it, what are the mechanics of that?" says art director Ocean Quigley. *Spore* provides the universe in a box, your own personal galaxy, which you can create and influence. The humble player starts the journey as a single-cell organism and travels an epic path from single cell to galactic god.

Little wonder, perhaps, that Will Wright refuses to conform to geek stereotype. His inspiration for *SimCity* came from an earlier game that allowed him to create his own maps during development. Wright found mapmaking both absorbing and intellectually satisfying. *SimCity* was born. At the time, Wright was reading a short story by Stanislaw Lem entitled "The Seventh Sally." In it, an engineer meets a deposed tyrant and creates a mini city with artificial citizens for him to oppress. The game was an instant hit with would-be tyrants and budding utopians alike.

"If anything, I'm more fascinated with reality than I am with games. Games just happen to be a convenient medium to express my fascination with reality I think most game designers are a little bit of the opposite; they have a fascination with games and player experience, and that's the primary motivation, and then they look for a theme to wrap that experience around," Wright explains. "For them, the play dynamic, the play experience, is almost the fundamental thing they are offering. I feel like I'm doing various paintings, caricatures of reality through the medium. For me, the medium is more of a tool and less my primary art form. I really enjoy bringing the concept to life, off the page. I think that's more than anything else what I try to convey in the games."

For *Spore,* Wright cherry-picked people from throughout the company. "The very best programmers are worth ten really good programmers," Wright calculates. "Programming is one of these things where there is an infinite number of ways of solving a problem. Typically there are a lot of straightforward ways, but hidden in there are a few very elegant solutions. If you can solve it in that elegant, simple way, what you end up with is a simple piece of code that anybody can understand. The people that can dig in and find that needle in a haystack, that incredibly elegant way of solving a problem, are perhaps ten times more valuable than those who go with the straightforward solution."

THE WRIGHT STUFF

What can we say about Will Wright? The first point is obvious: he is clever. Very clever. And clever in a way that is unique to him. You could scour the world (several worlds probably) and never find another with his perspective and creative talents.

The second point is that he has created enormous amounts of value for his organization, Electronic Arts. The *Sims* products have already earned millions of dollars for the company, and the brand franchise is worth many millions more. (In 2004, EA reported revenues of $2.96 billion—which the company said could be largely attributed to the *Sims* series and five other highly profitable product lines. In 2007, there were still five *Sims* products in the top ten PC retail games titles.)[2]

The third point is that, despite his enormous personal contribution to the bottom line, and in spite of the fact that he needs the support and infrastructure that EA provides, his primary affiliation is not with the company but with the project or cause. "You say Electronic Arts, but to me that doesn't have much meaning," he admits. His own start-up was one of those acquired by EA. As it has developed, EA has eschewed scale and centralization for a more flexible, smaller studio format. "I think they are finding that distributed studios that have more autonomy are going to give better results," Wright observes.

This is highly significant. Whether he likes it or not (and many clevers don't like it), Will Wright has a symbiotic relationship with EA. Thanks to the huge success of *Sims*, Wright is the star in Electronic Arts' creative firmament charged with turning *Spore* into the next blockbuster. He is, to all intents and purposes, a leader with a team of around one hundred followers.

Does Will Wright see himself as a leader? He shifts in his seat. Not uncomfortably but thoughtfully:

At some level, yes. I tend to see myself as one of the soft leaders. I'm more of a leader on the invisible wall chart and I much prefer to be that kind of a leader. I have been in roles where I was a manager and I had to write reports, and I found it very wearing and taxing emotionally. I feel like I'm more like the champion of the design vision. In some senses I'm carrying that flag. Occasionally somebody will come in and say that flag should be a different color, and we'll have an animated discussion and maybe we will choose to change the color or not. But I'm still the one holding the flag, and when somebody wants to come up and ask about the flag, I'm always the one who knows the current status, and I'll be the guardian of when they change or edit the flag. It's my job to get the flag to this destination. Around me are people with real organizational skills who understand other dimensions that I am blissfully ignorant of, things like the budgeting and scheduling. I see leadership in different dimensions.

In order to do what he does, Wright requires the company's commercial and financial muscle—everything from budgeting and scheduling to marketing and distribution. Without the EA machine, he could not bring *Spore* to the world.

The fourth point is that Wright's presence—and his almost legendary status in the industry—attracts other clevers and enables him to cherry-pick the very best talent to work on his project. This makes EA a magnet for the next generation of clevers in a way that no amount of expensive advertising, outlandish salaries, or corporate perks ever could. At a time when many talented computer-gaming professionals feel that too much money is invested in creating movie spin-off products rather than breakthrough games, this is an important statement.

Allied to this, the fifth, and final, point is that by channeling Wright into what he does best—creating highly innovative new computer games—EA is putting down a marker in the industry. It says, this is a company that believes in its people; this is a company that invests in those people and takes risks in pursuit of truly innovative products. More than that, it is actually very intelligent management. The choice with someone like Will Wright is either to let him do what he wants to do, or to reduce his value by narrowly involving him in the next *Sims* product extension. The reality is that his talents are better deployed in pushing the boundaries of gaming than in cranking a commercial handle.

Of course, past success is no guarantee of future success. As many a Hollywood backer knows, just because a director's last film was a hit does not preclude his or her next from being a flop—and an expensive flop at that. The same principles apply to computer games. Will Wright is the Steven Spielberg of his industry. That does not mean there is no risk attached to employing him. His high profile raises the stakes. To date, the signs look positive.

At the time of writing, *Spore* had been named by *Time* magazine as one of its best inventions of 2008. It had also scooped a number of awards—including Mobile Game of the Year, Best Family Game, and Best Artistic Design in the IGN Best of 2008 awards. But even if his next project is a flop (unlikely but not impossible), his contribution to EA and to the gaming industry will remain immense.

In fact, on the clever scale, Will Wright is probably as close as it gets to a perfect ten. Like him, the clever people we are concerned with in this book require a symbiotic relationship with an organization.

SYMBIOTIC MEN AND WOMEN

"If they didn't need the organization, why would they be here?" one CEO asked us. "They might not feel that they need the organization, and they might feel that they've got enough brains to do all sorts of other things, but the fact is, they stay. They feel they've got room to do what it is they need to do and that they might be vulnerable if they weren't in the organization. There is a protection element in the organization, even though they might hold it in contempt."

In organizational terms, the clever people we came across were needy. Understandably so. Looking at management innovation, our colleague Gary Hamel mirrors some of our thoughts in a typically poetical and powerful way. "No single individual can construct a jetliner, build a robust computer operating system, or make an Oscar-winning movie," says Hamel.

> "Once unleashed, human effort must be coordinated, and coordination tasks come in varying degrees of complexity. The simplest involves merely pooling resources—assembling a busload of farm laborers, for example, and delivering them to an orchard that needs pruning. At the other end of the spectrum is the challenge of optimizing the performance of a highly complex production system that requires the sequencing and integration of a varied mix of critical inputs. Improving the yields in a semiconductor factory, or better

managing risk in a global bank are examples of tasks that demand high levels of coordination."[3]

Complexity on a global scale demands coordination and clever people—and inspired leadership.

Clever people need their organizations. They may not always realize this fact, or be especially pleased about it, but it is true nonetheless. Herein lies a paradox that is at the heart of understanding and leading clever people (more about this later). Unlike the traditional company–employee relationship, where the individual follower is more dependent on the organization than the organization is on him or her, the relationship between a company and its clever people is a kind of interdependence between equals.

The challenge for leaders is to create the organization of choice for these people. How would you lead someone like Will Wright? Fail to do so, and you encourage them to walk into the open arms of your competitors. Succeed, and you tap into a vast reservoir of brilliant creativity and value generation. Increasingly, you cannot afford to fail.

The medical director of a hospital put the leadership dilemma like this: "Do I tolerate the cardiac surgeon who occasionally lobs his toys out the pram, and is a complete pain in the ass, because he's a fantastic cardiac surgeon? Or do I say, we wouldn't let a staff nurse on ward 22 behave like that; therefore, we're not going to let you behave like that? And my attitude is, I forgive them more than I forgive other people, but, in the process of doing so, every so often I remind them of this. It's an honest relationship. There is a line and it's important that they know there's a line, because those sorts of people will push you, and it becomes an intellectual exercise to see how far they can push you."

THE RISE OF THE CLEVER ECONOMY

Of course, people have been talking about the importance of star performers—and the shortage of such talent—for some time.[4] But we believe the situation is now becoming more acute. Knowledge is not an isolated or nice-to-have phenomenon; it is the essence of a myriad of jobs and the heart of modern national and corporate competitiveness.

"The world is changing," Ruben Vardanian, founding president of the Moscow School of Management Skolkovo, told us. "The question for leaders is how to create a system to attract the very best people. Because the main fight of the twenty-first century is not about assets. The main struggle in the nineteenth century was about the land. In the twentieth century, it was about industrial assets and natural resources. In the twenty-first century, the main challenge is to attract the best people. Because people need to believe they want to work for you, that they realize they can achieve their potential and meet their personal aspirations within the company."

Vardanian encapsulates (almost) everything we are talking about. He was instrumental in building Troika Dialog, the largest private investment bank in Russia. He joined the company in 1991, at the age of just 22, and became CEO in 1997 and chairman of the board in 2004. In 2006, he became the founding president of Skolkovo.

What was striking was how often leaders we talked to echoed Vardanian's sentiments. Some even matched his hospitality and personality. "We are in an industry where we have half the talent we need," estimated Bing Gordon of Electronic Arts. It didn't matter if they were hospital administrators in China or managers with American corporate giants like Cisco or Microsoft. No surprise, perhaps. Attracting talent has become something of a truism— like people being your greatest asset—but that does not make it any less true. How many leaders and organizations can truthfully meet Ruben Vardanian's challenge? How many have people who really want to work for the individual and the organization? How many believe they can realize their potential and meet their personal aspirations within your organization?

This contemporary drama has important ramifications in three vital areas: economic, sociological, and organizational. Indeed, we believe these three strands are closely interconnected.

Economically, intellectual know-how increasingly drives productivity, value creation, and growth. We are moving from a mass production system where the principal source of value was human labor to a new era where the principal component of value creation, productivity, and economic growth is knowledge. The scale of that transformation is only now becoming apparent.

In the industrial age the emphasis was on economies of scale—the idea was that bigger organizations could leverage their size to become more efficient. Today, for a growing number of companies, competitive advantage resides in the ability to *connect* ideas and know-how rather than simply achieving cost efficiencies.

Research by one of the leading global consulting firms, for example, estimates that "tacit" jobs—work involving complex interactions and a high level of expertise—now account for some 40 percent of the U.S. labor market, and a staggering 70 percent of the jobs created since 1998.[5] Forget McJobs, think clever jobs. A similar process is under way in other countries around the world. As companies become more reliant on their clever people, so are the old rules of business changing.

There are two clear implications of this change. The first is that intellectual capital—everything from patents and trademarks to software and ideas—has become a key source of value. The second is an increasing dependence within organizations on a small but growing number of clever people. Welcome (again) to the clever economy.

ECONOMIES OF IDEAS

The rise of what we call the clever economy is a phenomenon that recurred time and time again in our conversations with leaders and followers over the last five years. "There aren't economies of scale; there are economies of ideas," summarizes Werner Bauer, executive vice president, chief technology officer, and head of innovation, technology, and R&D at Nestlé, the world's largest foodstuffs manufacturer and the biggest industrial concern in Switzerland.

One of the most persuasive voices on the subject we encountered was Sir Martin Sorrell, chief executive of the world's biggest communications services company, WPP. Martin Sorrell is as forthright as he is imposingly well briefed. "The only reason for this company to exist," Sorrell told us matter-of-factly when we talked at WPP's London headquarters, "is to leverage economies of knowledge." He paused before adding, "One of the biggest challenges is that there are diseconomies of scale in creative industries. If you double the number of creative people, it doesn't mean you will be twice as creative."

Leveraging economies of knowledge is also high on the agenda of Franz Humer, chief executive and chairman of the Swiss-based pharmaceuticals giant Roche, which employs 68,000 people worldwide and sells its products in 150 countries. Humer and Sorrell are poles apart, in terms of their industries, styles, and personalities. Yet their comments to us echoed uncannily. "In my business of research, economies of scale don't exist. Globally today we spend $4 billion on R&D every year. But I could spend $9 billion, and my research wouldn't necessarily be any better; it could even be worse. I could spend $2 billion, but I don't know which $2 billion to take out," mused Humer, echoing the fabled comment about an organization not knowing which part of its marketing was working.[6]

FAST THIRST

What Bauer, Sorrell, and Humer are grappling with on a daily basis is a challenge that is central to economic and social progress in the twenty-first century: providing leadership to maximize human potential. The challenge is as old as civilization, but the scale of the issue is new. Today, our knowledge base renews itself more quickly than ever before. It is more delicately poised, more dynamic, and more lucrative than ever before.

Clever people are famous fast. Their impact is more profound and spreads more quickly than ever before. The global economy amplifies their influence. It has a thirst for speed and a talent for magnification. Will Wright is a computer-gaming brand in his own right. Jonathan Ive, the creator of the iMac, is (rightly) feted wherever he goes. Marc Jacobs at LVMH is garlanded with praise as the young designer who rejuvenated the Louis Vuitton brand. Think of Will Wright and the success of the *Sims* series—which is a truly global phenomenon. This simply would not have been possible thirty years ago. The good news about celebrity culture is that it makes celebrities out of clever people as well as Britney Spears et al.

Ideas, too, travel the world with unparalleled speed and ease. Ideas are unburdened by luggage and untroubled by customs formalities. Technological advances and the availability of information and communications technologies (ICT) both within organizations and outside have dramatically increased the speed with which new ideas and knowledge spread. Take a business book such as this. A book was once a one-dimensional slab of packaged words. Now it is a global product to be marketed, mined, and maximized. Its contents will be available in a range of formats: an article, a book in a variety of languages, a chapter download from Amazon, a podcast, a videocast, an e-pub, an Internet TV program. The world of ideas is open for business.

And there are other important changes. Within organizations and society, we can see the declining significance of hierarchy—as a means of getting things done in organizations and as an acceptable basis of authority. The old world was characterized by elaborate hierarchies, by more or less stable careers (for some, never for all), and by clear boundaries between organizations. Now, hierarchies in most organizations are becoming flatter, driven by the need for faster response times and by the competitive pressure to drive down costs. Hierarchies were not simply structural coordinating devices in organizations. Much more significantly, they were sources of meaning. As hierarchies flatten, the danger is that meaning—the raison d'être of working life—simply evaporates.

CLEVER MOVES

To this can be added incredible mobility—both geographical and social. When we run courses at London Business School or in Spain at IE Business School, they typically involve participants from twenty or more nations. One inspiringly peripatetic executive we talked to was originally from Bangladesh but had then been educated in Canada. From there, he had lived and worked in New York and then Japan—learning Japanese along the way—and is now working in London but would like to move to the West Coast. Such peripatetic lives are no longer unusual. Global comes as standard.

This means that careers for clever people are not a predictable and long climb through a single corporate hierarchy. They are far more likely to comprise a series of experiences, projects, and assignments across and between many flat and flexible organizations—often dispersed around the world. For them, a career is more of a smorgasbord than a plat du jour curling at the edges.

Our research shows that if you fail to grasp some basic insights and to follow several broad practices, you will push your most valuable resources into the open arms of your competitors. As one anonymous HR director put it, "I am a master of the dark arts of retention. I know about deferred options, elaborate tax plans, and all the paraphernalia of retention strategies. Let me tell you, none of these will work if the competition really wants your people. On the contrary, they will only stay if you can offer them a great place in which to express their cleverness and other clever people to work with." Even in companies that have high-compensation strategies for clever people, good promotion prospects, and exciting projects to work on, the difference between a high retention rate of the most talented and an average retention rate is in how they are led.

In an era of employee mobility, if you fail to engage your clever people intellectually and to inspire them with an organizational purpose, they will walk out the door. Are you opening that door by not presenting them with the opportunity to grapple with challenging problems?

The final ingredient affecting Planet Clever is the much-commented-on, but often elusive, search for work/life balance. People now demand a life as well as a career—not too much to ask when you think about it! They want freedom and flexibility rather than being shackled by organizational constraints. There is still a way to go. A regular stream of surveys reveals how people leave their imaginations and their happiness at home when they enter the workplace.[7] But the clever people we are talking about are not among them. They know their worth and expect to be rewarded accordingly. To a large extent, generous material rewards will be taken as a given. More important will be the sense of fulfillment and achievement that they are able to achieve through the work itself and the recognition that accompanies it.

CLEVERS MAKE THE COMPETITIVE DIFFERENCE

It is worth, at this point, inserting words of caution. The clever economy is not a utopian capitalist idyll. It is true that a team of pharmaceutical researchers who discover a new drug can potentially bankroll the entire organization for a decade. But clever people also have enormous destructive potential.

This can take its toll. We asked one leader how long he had been in a particularly testing job leading a technology team. He replied, "Physical years, I've been here two and a half years now.

Mental years, thirty-five. This is a beast to change; the challenges here are something I've never faced before. It is like turning the *Titanic*." (Muddling metaphors was the least of his worries.)

No one understands this dichotomy better than those who work in the academic world, which not only is a source of brilliant thinking but also can be rife with political maneuvering and dysfunctional behavior. Leading academics is notoriously demanding.

Tracey Horton had a successful career in consulting with Bain & Company in the United States. But she arrived as dean of the University of Western Australia Business School with a major challenge: to integrate the previously divided undergraduate and postgraduate management schools. She told us, "Highly talented people have the potential to create disproportionate amounts of value. They also have the potential to destroy disproportionate amounts of value. Sometimes individuals have egos such that they view their value as dwarfing the amount of value that others collectively offer, and behave accordingly, with their own set of rules. It may be true that their talent is significantly greater than any other individual in a team, but a team is dysfunctional if that attitude prevails."

Academia is not the only place such destructive behavior can be observed. Sometimes clevers can be too clever for their own good—and the good of the organization and its leaders. Investments can go down as well as up. That axiom also applies to clevers. You can invest in them, only to see that investment go up in smoke. As well as creating huge amounts of value when they get it right, clever people can—and frequently do—destroy huge amounts of value when they get it wrong. This can be bad for shareholders. It can also cost leaders their jobs.

We were reminded of this fact frequently as we were finishing this book. The much-vaunted credit crunch morphed into a full-blown banking crisis, which then required a series of massive government bailouts. Yet even these could not prevent an economic recession—of uncertain duration. The clever bankers who created the subprime mortgage market don't look so clever now. Some of them have lost their jobs—as have those who led them. Some of them have lost their banks! But we are all paying the price for their cleverness.

"What Were They Smoking?" was an early headline in *Fortune* magazine. The magazine went on to observe that the losses incurred were "shocking, because a pack of the highest paid executives on the planet, lauded as the best minds in business and backed by cadres of math whizzes and computer geeks, managed to lose tens of billions of dollars on exotic [financial] instruments built on the shaky foundation of subprime mortgages."[8]

Who were those math whizzes and computer geeks? Clever people, of course. But instead of creating value, as they intended, they ended up destroying value on an unprecedented scale.

As these examples illustrate, even the cleverest organizations make mistakes. From media to pharmaceuticals, no sector is exempt. The British Broadcasting Corporation (BBC) is full of clevers but was caught manipulating audience phone-in competitions and even managed to misrepresent an Annie Leibovitz photo session with the Queen as a royal tantrum rather than a costume change. Several pharmaceutical companies have had to recall drugs and take massive losses—think of Vioxx and Opren. In fact, the cleverer they are, the harder they can fall. Think of Jerome Kerviel at Société Générale. The actions of one clever person can decimate the results and standing of an entire organization—and even have an impact on worldwide markets. Lest we forget, Enron, too, was full of clever people.

Our experience suggests that there are lots of dysfunctional organizations full of clever people. We have worked with hospitals, consulting firms, legal practices, auditing firms, and many other organizations where we have emerged shaking our heads at the sheer bloody-minded dysfunctionality of people's behavior.

What determines whether an organization is a hub of clever collaboration or a toxic talent pool? We believe the answer lies with the quality of the leadership and the sense of moral purpose that it engenders. Our research suggests that how clevers are led makes a huge difference in whether their unquestionable—and often unstoppable—talents and energy are harnessed for good or allowed to fester. Time and time again, we have seen the difference effective leadership makes.

And we are sure that you, too, have observed this. You may have seen the difference a brilliant head teacher made to the performance of his teachers in your local school. Or how a well-led hospital dramatically improved on the quality of patient care. Or how a skillful chairman exploited the knowledge and experience of board members in a way that the predecessor had failed to do—with exactly the same personnel. Leadership counts.

So if, as Martin Sorrell suggests, the only reason for WPP and other organizations to exist is to leverage economies of knowledge, then the leadership challenge is to leverage the energy, inspiration, curiosity, and sheer intellectual chutzpah of clever people.

CHARACTERISTICS OF CLEVER PEOPLE

The question is, how do effective leaders make that difference? What is it that they do (or do not do) that channels the energy and ability of clever people in a positive direction—and one that creates value for all of the organization's stakeholders?

To lead clever people effectively, you have to do a number of things well. Chapter 2 examines those elements in detail. Here, though, we want to underline some general points. The starting line, if you are to effectively lead clever people, is to better understand their key characteristics. Unless you recognize their cleverness, you stumble at the first hurdle.

"What turns them on is to see what they've done in concrete results—a product, a process—the satisfaction of seeing their product or idea launched," says Werner Bauer at Nestlé. We asked Bauer what clever people get fed up about. "The first is when you kill ideas immediately. You can kill a whole team by a few words. The other thing is if you don't give people credit. Normally, the truly original ideas are found at the bench, not in management. Management should always give credit back to the guys at the bench. Sometimes you don't see the good ideas on paper. You see them in the eyes of the people when they fight for an idea, the sparkling in their eye when someone comes to you and says, 'Hey, shouldn't we do that?'"

One of our interviewees, Kamlesh Pande, is currently vice president of innovation and R&D at Thermax in Pune, India. He has extensive experience working in large Indian companies, including auto major Mahindra & Mahindra and has an impressive track record as a leader and a developer of clever people. Kamlesh speaks with passion and has a deep regard for the qualities of his colleagues; but he argues that clever people, at their most difficult, have the following characteristics:

- They take genuine pleasure and feel a sense of victory when they break any rule.

- They tend to trivialize the importance of nontechnical people.

- They are oversensitive about the projects they work on. The result is that they almost never agree to kill the projects they know are not leading anywhere.

- They suffer heavily from knowledge-is-power syndrome and seldom share their knowledge or contribute to knowledge management systems.

- They are never happy about the review/evaluation process they and their projects are subjected to. However, if they are asked to come up with one that will satisfy a majority, they are largely clueless.

Although they are extreme, to a large extent we agree with these points. We were also amused by Martin Sorrell's observation that "if you want to get people to do things, you always say the opposite. If I want people to go left, they will always go right. So I've figured it out that if I say, 'Go right,' I'll get them to go left. Particularly in our industry, which is a creative professional services industry, there is a great difficulty in trying to get people to move in the same direction at the same point in time."

Even so, we felt impelled to develop our own clever identity kit. Not every clever person has all of the following characteristics. Cleverness must always be contextualized. But our research suggests that there are a number of important attributes of clever people. Though the following list is not exhaustive, we identified nine common characteristics.

1. **Their cleverness is central to their identity.** For clever people, what they do is not some last-minute career choice; it is who they are, rooted deep in their being. Louise Makin is CEO of the pharmaceutical company BTG plc; she has an MBA, an MA in natural sciences, and a PhD in metallurgy from Cambridge University. "The thing about experts is, they *are* their work," she notes

   Listen to how people introduce themselves. Clever people will say that they're physicists, geneticists, film producers, software designers, and so on. They do not say, "I work for Clever Inc." They are defined by their passion, not their organization.

   "In every organization I've seen, it is the people who follow their passion who do best," says the partner of a leading global consulting firm. "Their passion encourages followership among colleagues and can rally people around a cause. They excel at what they do because they're in the bathroom in the morning thinking about what they're going to be doing in the day, because they just love it."

   This means that clever people may become obsessive about their current project. It means everything. Of course, this may have personal and financial side effects. "Sometimes they don't get the 80/20 rule," Julie McEver laments. McEver—a smart, MBA-educated American—works with expert researchers in the London offices of New Philanthropy Capital, which focuses on maximizing the impact of donors and charities. They do this through independent research, creating tools for charities, and giving advice to donors. It is staffed largely with high performers from a variety of backgrounds, including financial services, corporations, management consultancies, academia, and government, as well as charities, trusts, and foundations. In some respects, it's the archetypal clever organization of the twenty-first century, servicing a new moneyed niche as well as charities. "It's hard enough to get my people to think about 100 percent; they're working to 150 percent. They read every piece of literature about their topic, and that means pages and pages of government policy documents," says McEver.

An unfortunate side effect of such obsession is that clevers find it hard to shut off—or to keep to a schedule if it means not finishing a task to their satisfaction. "You get some people who tell you their timelines, and every time, it shifts by two more weeks," she says. "When I say that can't be happening, they look at me with blank stares and say why not?"

They say why not because clever people want to leave no stone unturned. They are perfectionists—even if their budgets have failed to cost out perfection.

The close association between what they do and who they are also means that clever people often see themselves as not being dependent on others. The leader must, therefore, start by acknowledging their independence and difference. If leaders do not do this, they fail at first base. But, and it is an important caveat, the leader's job is to make them understand their interdependence. Recognizing the symbiotic nature of the relationship is critical to both the individual and the organization.

It can be a hard sell. Interdependence only goes so far. Clever people are so focused on their professional passion that the bigger picture can be immaterial to them. Clever people tend to be extraordinarily interested in whatever they are clever in. This can mean that if you try to explain where their part fits into the overall picture—of how the users are going to use it—they say, that's interesting, but why are you bothering me with it? The leader can end up constantly checking that people aren't creating incredibly elegant computer systems that are of little or no use to the end user. With clevers, their own sense of beauty can become a money-consuming beast. They start off designing a cup, and you end up with a tea set. "Creeping elegance!" snorted one CEO we talked with.

Another corollary of this identification with what they do is that making the leap to a more general leadership role is often highly demanding for clever people. They have a lot to give up, and the career gains may not be immediately apparent.

Jane Collins, for example, qualified as a doctor and then trained to be a hospital consultant. She became a pediatric consultant at Guy's Hospital, London, and then moved to the world-famous children's hospital at Great Ormond Street, where she is now chief executive. Great Ormond Street is the United Kingdom's national center of excellence in children's health care. It has over three hundred doctors and nine hundred nurses and health-care assistants who look after around one hundred thousand patients and perform over five hundred heart operations on children every year.

We asked Jane Collins about leading the clever people who fulfill the difficult and challenging medical roles at her hospital. "Well, I suppose I do understand them because I was one of them. I am a doctor, and I have an idea of how they see the world," she mused. "But very importantly, I realized on day one as chief executive, I was no longer one of them. It was history. When I decided to become a chief executive, the thing which bothered me was giving up my identity of being a doctor. It is very deeply bound up with how you see yourself. Interestingly now, I rarely refer to myself as a doctor, and that's happened quite quickly. I realized that I was not one of them, because when you are chief executive, you are separate and, of course, you're separate from your executives really, in a way, as well. So it's important that you don't mind that."

Collins's insight is a good one. She recognized that in order to be an effective leader, she had to step away from her identity as a doctor. That is not to say that she is not still proud of her profession or that she does not use her qualification when appropriate. Rather, it is the fact that she is aware of the tension between being a clever and being part of an organization. Her awareness of the issue allows her to skillfully deploy her membership in the medical clever tribe to best effect. Yet, for many of the clevers we met, the tension between their affiliation with their clever profession or discipline and their employer remained unresolved and uncomfortable. This can have a profound impact on how they relate to the organization.

Put simply, they are obsessive perfectionists by nature. This makes them resistant to relying on others—especially those in whom they do not recognize the same sort of cleverness. This engenders a fierce sense of independence—and even hostility—toward the rest of the organization. This in turn makes them resistant to any move that might threaten their clever identity. Of course, this includes the transition into a management or leadership role.

2. **Their skills are not easily replicated.** If they were, then they would not be the scarce resource they are. Once upon a time, competitive advantage came because your product was slightly better or produced more cheaply. Now it often comes through the collective efforts of the people in your organization. The good thing about people—and the teams they create—is that they are (as yet) impossible to copy.

   You can practice twelve hours a day, but you will not become an identical soccer player to David Beckham. Nor will you create a great team just by buying the best individual players. This was expensively demonstrated by the Spanish soccer team Real Madrid, which invested many millions of euros in a team of *galacticos,* superstar players including Zinadine Zidane, Roberto Carlos, Ronaldo, Raul, and David Beckham. The sum of the glittering parts was disappointing.

   The knowledge of clever people is tacit. It is embedded in them. If it were possible to capture their knowledge within the organizational fabric, then all that would be required would be better knowledge management systems. It isn't. (In fact, as alluded to by Kamlesh Pande, one of the great disappointments of knowledge management initiatives to date is their failure to capture clever knowledge.) For the people we are talking about, a great deal of their cleverness resides not in *what* they know but *who* they know and *how* they know it.

   Indeed, as noted above, their profession or discipline is typically a lot more important to many of them than the particular organization that happens to currently employ them. Thus, they value professional networks above organizational networks—and hierarchies. They are more concerned about what their peers in another organization think of them than what their boss thinks.

   The fact that they understand that their knowledge is both hard to replicate and a function of the professional networks they belong to is linked to the next characteristic.

3. **They know their worth.** Kamlesh Pande is now responsible for a
   group of around forty R&D people. The majority are post-
   graduates in engineering. Some are engineering graduates,
   and a smaller number have doctorates in engineering.
   Pande recounted a recent experience when he had interviewed a candidate for a job. The job applicant was from the
   same institute that he himself had graduated from and was
   clearly exceptionally talented. Pande immediately offered
   him the salary that he wanted—around 25 percent higher
   than he would normally have offered—and invited him to
   join the company when he finished his PhD. The candidate
   agreed to join—but on one condition. He insisted on having
   a look at his workplace to see how well equipped the lab was
   and meeting at least four or five people he was going to
   work with. Pande agreed and celebrated the fact that India is
   now producing people with such high expectations and
   standards.

   Indeed, the tacit skills of clever people are closer to the
   craft skills of the medieval period than they are to the codifi-
   able and communicable skills that characterized the Industrial Revolution.[9] This means you can't transfer the
   knowledge without having the people. Clever people know
   the value of this.

   While some of the clever people we interviewed were reti-
   cent and unsure of the dynamics of their relationships with
   their leaders, many more expressed a sureness, a confidence
   in their own skills and their role in the organization. "I believe in openness," a senior scientist told us. "I think we all
   come to work here trying to do the best job, and sometimes
   we don't. This is what I really appreciate with my boss,
   who's very open. He tells you, look, this was not well done,
   this could have been better, you go and try and improve.
   So I like to be led in a very open way in terms of where
   my strengths are, where my weaknesses are, and what

additional support I need to get better. That's very important for me. The other thing is that I like people to give me
room to do what I have to do. That is not something that
happens overnight, but I've been around for a while and I
understand the company. I know what I have to do."

Such sentiments represent an important power shift.
Confident in their own worth and ability, clever people
exert pressure on their leaders. Their skepticism about the
value of leadership puts pressure on leaders to demonstrate
their worth.

At the Formula One auto-racing team, McLaren Racing,
managing director Jonathan Neale talks of the collective
high standards, which apply to him as much as to the engineers and technicians. "There is a lot of peer pressure here,"
he says. "Pressure in the organization is brought about by a
sense of competitiveness and collective responsibility. People who are held in high regard make a difference. Here, it's
often informally referred to as 'getting the job done.' That
phrase is used a lot. 'That guy can be relied on to get the job
done,' is one of our core values about winning and working
together. Can you be relied upon to get the job done?"
Imagine if the people who work with you asked the same
question. Do you know their likely answer?

The fact that they can be as blunt about their leaders
speaks volumes about how clevers see themselves and their
organizations. If, as a leader, you cannot be relied upon to
help them get the job done, then why would they listen to
you? Why are you even bothering them? Indeed, the fact
that they are sufficiently engaged to challenge the leader is
a good clue to whether the leader is doing a good job. This
highlights another important characteristic.

4. **They ask difficult questions.** "My clearest indication that I have
somebody who is really talented is that they will come into

my office and argue with me on some issue where they are convinced they're right. The fact that they are passionate enough to sit and argue with me is a huge indicator," says Will Wright. "It doesn't matter how talented a designer is, if they can't come and sell me on their ideas, it's wasted. I have others who come in and argue, and they are always wrong! So, it's not necessarily a proof that they are a great design talent, but I think it is a prerequisite."

Knowing your worth means that you are more willing to challenge and question. Clever people are often incessant interrogators of those who hope to lead them. But Will Wright's point is also deceptive. The fact that they are prepared to argue with someone of his stature is significant. It is a sign of respect for him as a leader. Not every leader can rely on retaining that respect. But if you have it, you should not expect an easy ride from the clevers.

There are many examples where the willingness to challenge assumptions and cherished beliefs has led to breakthrough innovations. As the political theorist Thomas Hobbes said when asked why he gave short shrift to the literature, "If I had only read what others have written then I would only know what they knew."

Clevers instinctively challenge what came before them. This isn't pigheaded questioning for the sake of it. Indeed, clever people begin by questioning themselves. Rob Murray, CEO of Lion Nathan, put it this way: "I came into my career, looked at the pyramid in front of me, and wanted to climb to the top of that pyramid. Interestingly, having got to the top of the pyramid, you reappraise yourself. These people, being really clever, have got to that question before I did."

In the beginning is a question. Often it may seem a naive question. Yet, this is another misleading aspect of dealing with clevers. They may seem organizationally inept, but they are effective at getting what they want. Think of them as people who are able to see how a game works and then use that knowledge to win. Naive bystanders? We don't think so.

5. **They are organizationally savvy.** Says Will Wright, "In my experience clever people understand organizational dynamics, politics, etcetera. You do not want to entirely isolate them from the political pressures, the disciplinary dynamics going on around them. If you are going to protect them, you want them to be aware of that. We're giving you some space here; we are holding back the managers, and it's costing you brownie points; and if you do something really cool, you earn brownie points. They very much understand the balance of payment, and they are happy thinking in those terms. In my experience they are very open to understanding that as a marketplace."

   It is easy to assume that clever people are organizational innocents, too focused on their own expertise to play political games. The reality is somewhat different. They are human—and clever with it. Clever people will find the organizational context where their interests will be most generously funded. When the funding dries up, they have several options. They can move on to somewhere where resources are plentiful; or they can dig in and engage in elaborate organizational politics to ensure that their pet projects are indulged. This is a pattern we have witnessed over and over in academic and research-based organizations. They are expert gamers.

6. **They are not impressed by corporate hierarchy (and they don't want to be led).** The demands of the clever economy pose a leadership conundrum. We describe it as a conundrum for a simple reason: if there is one defining characteristic of clever people, it is that they claim they do not want to be led—and they are absolutely certain that they don't want to be managed.

As noted earlier, clevers are also more concerned with what their professional peers think of them than their boss. They have an undisguised disdain for organizational hierarchy as captured in the organizational chart.

Their indifference to organizational hierarchy has important implications for leading them. "You are only as good as your last idea," summarizes Christina Kite of the technology company Cisco Systems. "It's all about influencing through skill and knowledge, not through title, especially in engineering. They don't give a hoot what title you have. You've got to influence them through your skill and your knowledge, and your brand, because they'll ask around. At the end of the day, they're a show-me-don't-tell-me group."

Louise Makin agrees. "You have to lead as *you*. You don't lead as the CEO," she cautions.

Another important point to recognize is that clevers will not follow a leader; the best leaders understand that all they can hope to do is to guide them—gently—in the desired direction. As Saul Van Beurden, head of company-wide operations and IT transformation at the financial services company ING, put it, "Clever people need to have respect for the one who is guiding them. You can build that by being authentic. It helps if you can show them the way, not too much but enough to steer them in the right direction. If you roll it out for them, it's not theirs anymore. You have to give them hunches, finger points, certain directions."

Clevers can be anywhere on an old-fashioned organization chart. Unlike some who are driven to reach the top, they may not be hierarchically aspirational—indeed, many clever people are resistant to the notion. Leaders who seek to use titles or hierarchical promotion to motivate them are likely to be met with cold disdain. (Interestingly, however, they may have their own unofficial organizational hierarchy—what Will Wright described earlier as "the invisible wall chart.")

This also means they are likely to be motivated by factors other than money and power. But don't make the mistake of assuming this means clever people don't care about status or recognition. Their reference points tend to be outside the organization—with their profession or their clients. Clever people can be very particular about their professional status and may insist on being called doctor or professor.

It is also worth noting a cultural difference here. In India, for example, hierarchy is very deeply rooted in families, society, and organizational life. This means that feedback may not be easily accepted from a clever person regarded as lower down in the hierarchy.

7. **They expect instant access.** The ideas of clever people are so all-consuming to them that they cannot understand why they may not be to their leaders as well. If they don't get access to the chief executive, they will assume that the organization does not take their work seriously.

"Their ideas are so present to them now that they cannot understand why they may not be present to you—*now!*" summarizes Laura Tyson, reflecting on her experience as chief economic adviser in President Clinton's first administration and latterly as dean of London Business School. So perhaps it's not surprising that many of WPP's clever people perceive Martin Sorrell's legendary speed of response to e-mails (within a few minutes most of the time) as one of the most distinctive and valued aspects of his leadership style. The challenge for leaders is to balance open access with what might be regarded as interference.

The trouble for you, as the leader, is that if you're not there when the clevers come calling, don't expect them to wait patiently in line; clever people have a low boredom threshold. Very low.

At EA, Will Wright calculates that with a team of twenty people, three hours was usually spent working for every one hour spent on meeting and coordinating. Of course, as numbers increase, the dynamic of meeting time and productivity almost reverses. With eighty people, three-hour meetings tend to yield an hour of work. In response, Wright keeps an eye on who is invited to a meeting, how long the meeting lasts, and how it's run. Some team members are strong enough to leave as soon as they feel it has delivered what they need. "Do you need me anymore?" is a frequently heard and well-mannered exit line. Clever people are loath to hang around in needless meetings or to waste time when they could be focusing on cracking a thorny problem.

8. **They want to be connected to other clever people.** We have already made the point that clever knowledge cannot easily be downloaded to the organization. Indeed, it is almost always inseparable from the clever people themselves. But here is that paradox again. Just as organizations need clever people to be effective, so, too, do clever people need other clever people—and organizations—to achieve their full potential.

In part, this has to do with access to resources. But that is not the whole story. It also has to do with the fact that clever people cannot function in an intellectual vacuum. Typically, they possess only a part of the clever solution—an important part, perhaps, but one that also requires the input of other clevers to come to life. Think of Will Wright at EA. Does he have all the necessary expertise to conceptualize, program, design, price, manufacture, package, market, and distribute *Spore* all on his own? Unlikely. And even if he did, unless people buy and use his games, there is no point to his cleverness.

Clever people need others; they need organizations to plug into. Their concern with professional status usually means that clever people are plugged into highly developed knowledge networks—as we said earlier, *who* they know is often as important as *what* they know. Cleverness is socially confirmed in interactions with others. Their strong external networks both increase their value and make them more of a flight risk for the organization.

As clever people enjoy networking with like-minded or like-qualified individuals, one of the challenges to the leader is to create internal networks, which satisfy their professional and developmental needs.

This point was made clear when we talked to Werner Bauer of Nestlé. As he told us:

> You have to establish a prosperous network of knowledge. When I was head of research for Nestlé, that was the first thing I established across functional boundaries. My argument was that what we know in one area could inspire new ideas in another.
>
> For example, our low-temperature-freezing ice cream—now launched in the U.S. and Europe—has half the calories of traditional ice cream. Our goal originally was to have a low-calorie ice cream—something you cannot do with normal technologies. The material scientists said, if we do an extrusion of ice cream at minus temperatures, then we could perhaps create a low-fat ice cream. Until that point, the extruder people had only thought about hot processes, cereal extrusion, plastic extrusion, and so on. Nobody had ever thought of bringing an extrusion into the ice cold, and through this bringing about a revolution in ice cream.

Today, Nestlé has a food science and technology knowledge network with fourteen subgroups. Each of these has a leader who has no line responsibility over any of the people in the network. The leaders are normally drawn from one of the company's R&D centers. Their role as leader is to bring together the knowledge of all the people in Nestlé who have know-how in that area.

For clever people, networking is not a social nicety but a source of perpetual improvement and bright ideas. Networks enable clever people to question assumptions and to make previously unacknowledged links. Unacknowledged links are also the topic of the final clever characteristic we have observed.

9. **They won't thank you.** "There's a part of me, a slightly dark part of me, that thinks these clever people wouldn't recognize management or leadership if you hit them in the face with it," one slightly forlorn leader confided. This may be true, but it also gets to the heart of the challenge. Clever people might retort that leaders wouldn't easily recognize great science, a world-changing computer program, or even an innovative new coffee machine if it was thrust before them.

Others we spoke to were more philosophical. One interviewee put it like this: "If clever people resist leadership, it is the fault of the leader rather than the clever person. Furthermore, if clever people resist management, almost invariably most others in the organization have similar concerns."

Even when you're leading them well, clever people may be unwilling to recognize your leadership. In the next chapter, we'll look at what effective leadership involves. But remember, these clever individuals will often say that they don't need to be led. Measure your success by your ability to remain on the fringes of their radar. You know you're a success when you hear them say you're not getting in the way too much.

WHAT CAN LEADERS DO?

T HE GROWING IMPORTANCE of clevers in the knowledge economy poses a huge challenge for organizations. Our research suggests that leading clever people requires a very different style of leadership from that traditionally seen in many organizations. In our experience, getting the best from clevers requires many of the traditional leadership virtues, such as excellent communications skills and authenticity. But it also requires leaders to demonstrate some additional qualities.

The need for nontraditional leadership skills was emphasized again and again among the leaders and followers we talked to. "Managing clever people is a nightmare because you're not managing them, you're guiding them, you're being a mentor, you're stroking their ego, you need to do all of these types of things," one leader told us. The command and control leadership guidebook does not have a chapter on ego stroking!

"Throughout my career, I've worked with very smart people at Bankers Trust, Merrill Lynch, and General Motors," observes Neil Buckley, a senior IT executive at ING, who adds:

> The big issue is how much empowerment you give these
> clever people. You can't day-to-day manage them. You don't

want to manage them. You really want to keep them focused on deliverables and on the end target. With clever people, that is a very hard steering job.

They always deliver, but they play their own game and sometimes they go their own route. You might not know how they're going to hit, and you might not understand their journey, but if they're empowered and you have the confidence and the trust that they're going to get there, you have to take that leap of faith. You manage them by providing a route and guidance, and measurable steps along the way. If you try to put someone in that's going to manage them, they'll switch off.

LEADING WITH A LIGHT TOUCH

One of the recurring factors in our research was the language effective leaders used to describe their role with clevers. It was about "trust, guidance, support, listening, closeness, being valued, sharing values, parenting, helping, nurturing, creating the right atmosphere," and so on. At first we wondered whether these were simply euphemisms for more traditional leadership behaviors, or whether our interviewees were especially adept at what are perceived as the soft skills. In the end we decided it was neither. What these leaders were doing was expressing their genuine belief about their role as leaders using a vocabulary that they have found clevers are receptive to. That does not mean that they are pushovers. Far from it. Often there was a steely edge to them that said, "You can push this far but no farther."

"Clevers need to know where the limits are," one leader told us. "Otherwise, there will be anarchy—and that is not good for anyone." Leaders were also clear that once the line was crossed, they had to take swift and uncompromising action. Not for them the knee-jerk reaction to having their authority challenged. Rather, the iron will to act in the best interests of the organization.

These are clever leaders. They are also not overly encumbered with hubris. It was notable among the leaders we interviewed that the most successful were powerful, intelligent, and impressive people, but people with their egos firmly and confidently in check.[1] They practiced humility for a purpose.

Take Marc Silvester, chief technology officer of Fujitsu Services. We asked him how he sees his job in leadership terms:

> My job is to work together with our other managers to lead the transformation of our business as it transforms our customers' business. With that comes all of the highlights and lowlights: the nitty-gritty stuff—products, services, and offers that need to be there—and occasionally through to the political aspects of leading through change, bringing together parts of the organization, identifying known and unknown agendas, and convincing and assisting people to make the change. You could dress all that up and say it's strategy, or you could say that it's a technology leadership role. It isn't, really; it's just a familiar, trustworthy face that works within the organization to bring together good people to do good things for an agenda.

Indeed, the most effective leaders we talked to were highly conscious of how they appeared to those they led. Says Louise Makin:

> You've got to have that humility. You've got to be big enough when you need to be big enough—and small enough when you need to be small. They [clever people] want to know that somewhere out there, there's somebody fighting on behalf of the company. So my job is to support and coach, and make sure people will go for as long as they possibly can, and that I've got the right people coming in.
>
> Every time you go into a room, you have to ask yourself, what role am I here to play, because there are so many different

roles as a CEO. Often you're playing a set piece—you're there as the CEO if you're in some sort of corporate negotiation or you're a sort of figurehead with an investor. It's who you are as a person that will make people follow you, and I spend a lot of time trying to keep myself in a good spot to do difficult things like listen to the silences, have really good judgment, get that right balance of loose and tight. You have to be really on good form to do that, and you have to know yourself well enough.

It is worth highlighting an important shift here. Leading clever people requires a degree of humility that goes beyond that required in traditional organizations. "I'm not going to talk about leadership actually. That's really for others to judge. And it would be precocious and pretentious for me to talk about it," responded Martin Sorrell, bridling when asked to fulminate on his leadership style. Indeed, discomfort with the subject of leadership is commonplace among the leaders we talk to. They are uneasy with setting themselves apart, of setting themselves up as somehow better.

"I want people to value me and respect me for what I am rather than thinking simply that operating on people's brains is rather special," says medical leader and neurosurgeon Peter Lees.

There is something reassuringly downbeat and genuine about such observations. Our experience is that people who revel in being *a leader* tend not to be very effective. Leading clevers is not about knowing more than those you lead. Nor is it about outsmarting them. This perhaps surprising humility plays out in two ways.

First, there are leaders who have thought long and hard about what they actually bring to the clever party. They have a degree of confidence in what they stand for, and how their perspective and experience differs and adds value. They know exactly what they bring to the party—and so does everyone they lead.

"What I bring is discipline, process, a sense of timescale, what I want by when, but then enthusiasm and vision about where we have to take our business and the part that they play in the picture and why that's important," explains a senior woman in a large, global pharmaceutical consulting firm. "I think they're really clever, a damn sight cleverer than I am, but they'll never get there if you just let them figure it out for themselves. They would go off and go down different routes that interested them."

We talked to some of the leaders at Electronic Arts overseeing the work of the likes of Will Wright. David Gardner ran EA's studios outside the United States and had worked with the company since its early days. Interestingly, he saw himself as the repository of what the company stands for. "I bring a conviction of our company values, and I bring the DNA, the history of the company from the beginning, and I bring a different leadership style that is compatible with the kind of people we need in the company. I don't bring any technical ability. I think it's surprisingly hard for a company to hold on to its values ahead of hitting their numbers."

We also talked with EA's chief creative officer, William "Bing" Gordon. A Yale drama and literature major, Gordon waited tables at Max's Kansas City, acted off-Broadway, did an MBA at Stanford, worked at the advertising firm Ogilvy and Mather, and in 1982 became one of the earliest EA employees, starting off as *the* marketing department.

"Most answers to leadership also work for parenting," Gordon observes. "There is the Stalin way of parenting: 'Do what I say or I'm going to ground you.' One of my favorites is a parent who said, 'Age twelve, you get to make 10 percent of your decisions, at age twenty-one you get to make 100 percent of your decisions, so let's increase by 10 percent every year,'" he recounts. "My own philosophy to lead people that are smarter than me is to find ways for them to be more productive in what they want to do. Sometimes that's to give them new facts. Managing is a well-known power trade-off; in leadership it is not clear what's in it for the leader. With management you get slaves, you get a bigger office, and you get paid more. Leadership is not clear unless the leader is also part of a team. If that's the case, leadership is about your team doing better."

A recurring theme among other interviewees was that the leader sets the tone and adds some sort of discipline, structure, or sense of process to the organization. "The value that I add is twofold," says Kamlesh Pande. "One is creating an atmosphere for these people to sustain their cleverness and to ensure that they don't fall sideways into mediocrity. The second thing is aligning what the organization wants and what they want to do. If I align at least 50 percent of these two things, I think my job is done. But then the rest of my job is about convincing them and following them and going after them. My job is to create a strategy or an atmosphere where I align what these clever people want to do and what the organization wants. The rest is easy."

We are cautious about formulaic answers to complex questions. But our research leads us to a simple conclusion: leading clever people requires humility *and* toughness. Either alone is insufficient.

LISTEN TO THE SILENCES

But while some leaders were very clear (and candid) about what they offered, other very clever leaders had not reached definitive answers about what they brought to the party. But they were effective because they were good at tuning in to colleagues, sensing the context, and then responding appropriately. For some leaders, it is a keen awareness of playing a distinctive leadership role. For others, it is more an ability to tune in to and respond to changing context. But whichever form it takes, this sense of awareness of the changing situation is an important issue and one that has recurred throughout our leadership research. We call it *situation sensing,* and the most effective leaders we have seen do it all the time—consciously or unconsciously.

These leaders recognize that what people tell you will only get you so far. You must also listen to the silences. University leader Sir Graeme Davies told us that when he ran one university, he was in the habit of taking an evening walk. As he strolled the campus, he found it an illuminating experience in more ways than one. Obviously, he bumped into people and started useful, unplanned conversations. Leaders can become isolated from the clever people working for them. He also noticed which departments had their lights on late at night and were still working. There was a correlation between activity levels and the quality of the outputs.

All leaders must adapt to context. But in order to adapt, it is necessary to first sense the situation. One of the leaders we talked to modestly kept some of his qualifications from his team (humility with a purpose). While he has a degree in the technology used by his company, he also has additional degrees in another science and psychology. He credits his psychology studies with a huge impact on his leadership style, but does not necessarily want his team members knowing of his expertise as it might intimidate them. "The biggest strength it gives you is empathy, an instinctive way of wanting to listen and understand, and then to work on things from the perspective of people. So it is not just a trite matter of sitting there for ten minutes listening, and then spending the next ninety minutes telling them what you think the answer is. It's an inherent way of looking at it completely from their perspective, and then stepping away from that one or two times to wrap it up and then to go back behind it and help them move themselves forward in the way in which they are thinking."

Another leader was similarly coy about his MBA. "I've never mentioned my MBA to anybody since I've been here, because it has connotations of processing engineering, with tea, toast, and toilet managing. I don't do soft furnishings!"

We explored the idea of listening to silences with EA's Will Wright. "When you put different people on a project, they all have different models of what's going to happen and what they are going to be doing in their imagination," he says. "Usually, that silence, in my experience, occurs when the reality they are confronted with does not match their model, and they are trying to figure out should I reformulate my model or is reality going in the wrong direction?"

Clearly, being sensitive to such gaps between expectations and reality is an important part of the leader's role. Allowed to develop unchecked, such gaps can become chasms.

TUNING IN TO LEADERSHIP

Leading clevers requires an ability to tune in to their context: to view the world through their eyes. This requires leaders with well-developed antennae to pick up faint signals that others might miss. We call this ability *situation sensing*. It is made up of observational and cognitive skills. Leaders see and sense what's going on and then use their cognitive skills to interpret these observations. They pick up and interpret soft data—sometimes without any verbal explanation. For example, they sense when a team is on task and on target or when additional resources are required.

The process is subtle—so much so that it is not always easy to "see" it. But there are some key moments when you may often observe this skill—or its absence—in workplace interactions. Think of meetings, for example, when someone joins late and immediately wants to take control. This kind of behavior typically reflects "negative" situation sensing. Others seem to be able to join a meeting and immediately tune in—effortlessly picking up on atmosphere or ambience. (In our experience, this is especially rare in meetings with clevers.)

Highly task-oriented executives very often neglect the basic observational work. They rush into action before fully understanding the situation—sometimes with very negative consequences. When these people are dealing with clevers, the negative impact of such behavior can be disastrous, leading to a total breakdown in communication.

TABLE 2-1

Dos and don'ts for leading clevers

Dos	Don'ts
Explain and persuade	Tell people what to do
Use expertise	Use hierarchy
Give people space and resources	Allow them to burn out
Tell them what	Tell them how
Provide boundaries (agree on simple rules)	Create bureaucracy
Give people time	Interfere
Give recognition (amplify their achievements)	Give frequent feedback
Encourage failure and maximize learning	Train
Protect them from the rain	Expose them to politics
Give real-world challenges with constraints	Build an ivory tower
Talk straight	Use bull or deceive
Create a galaxy	Recruit a star
Conduct and connect	Don't take all the credit as the leader

Communicating with clevers is always a challenge because they are totally absorbed by their own agendas. Engaging with them in a way that means they see the leader as being on their side is vital.

To lead clever people effectively, you have to do a number of things well. A sense of humility and sensitivity to context are the foundations. In addition, the leader must use a light touch. As a result of our observations, we have identified a number of dos and don'ts that apply to leading clevers (see table 2-1).

EXPLAIN AND PERSUADE

Clever people do not like to be told what to do—and are likely to react badly if they are. Needing to be told seems to undermine their sense of self-esteem—clever people shouldn't need telling!

So the art of leadership begins with listening and talking—and lots of it. This is leadership by conversation, not by edict.

After university, Alison Fields spent three years working as a researcher with the U.S. Army and then spent the rest of her career working in information technology and knowledge management in the federal government. "Clever people tend to require more explanation of your decisions and more persuasion than ordinary employees," she says. "I spent an enormous amount of time explaining and persuading. On the other hand, I had to do much less orienting [of] people to their jobs, training them on their jobs, or giving them any guidance on how to do their jobs. They required, by and large, less feedback than most employees in how they were doing on a day-to-day or month-to-month basis."

ING's Neil Buckley agreed. "Clever people want to work in an environment of trust," he told us. "The other thing is, they don't like to be told *no*. What they respect is if people say no, with an explanation. When it comes to communication from senior management, they are high maintenance. You have to explain more; they don't take no or yes for an answer."

In the clever economy, command and control is ancient history. Yes, really. If you have spent ten years in banking and find yourself running a pharmaceutical company, you have a lot to learn and a lot of skeptical clever people to tune in to and learn from. For a nonspecialist to accurately gauge the context in an environment populated by clever people requires highly acute situation-sensing skills—that is, the ability to judge morale, commitment, and individual motivation—in an area where the leader's knowledge base is already stretched.

USE EXPERTISE

Hierarchy, of course, still exists. There are CEOs, CFOs, CIOs, department heads, and so on. But using hierarchy to justify decisions or behavior is dangerous and probably self-defeating. This applies throughout the leader's behavior. Clevers will respond far better to *expert* power than to *hierarchical* power.

As in so many other ways, Will Wright is exceptional. He is a leader who is also an acclaimed expert among the clever people he leads. "In most contexts where you have a very specialized skill set and talented and extremely intelligent people, your boss is dumber than you. Will is one of the rare cases where I have all those things, but Will is actually smarter than me. Thankfully I have some knowledge that is not parallel to his, so I can trump him with specifics, but he is a hard man to bamboozle," admits Ocean Quigley.

Most leaders of clevers have more in common with Quigley's situation than Wright's. They cannot hope to be as clever as the clevers they lead. Their job is to enable their clevers to reach their potential. In some cases this will translate into a form of servant leadership. As with Quigley, however, it helps if they have knowledge or expertise that is not parallel to that of their followers.

Clever people do not expect that their leader's knowledge should match their own unique and specialist know-how. But they do expect that the leader is clearly and demonstrably an expert in their own field. Sometimes the knowledge is in a similar or related field of expertise; other times it is completely distinct. We call the first type of expertise supplementary—because it supplements what they know. The second type we call complementary expertise—because it not in the same field but it is recognized by them as valuable. Either can work, but a leader needs one or the other. "You must be good at something, or they won't give you floor space—and do it quick!" advises Mary Edwards, the CEO of Basingstoke and North Hampshire NHS Foundation Trust, part of the United Kingdom's National Health Service (NHS).

Demonstrating their critical competence is a key leadership role. Leaders have to prove themselves to the clever people they lead. It is about gaining their respect. Remember, these people are not impressed by hierarchy, so simply being the boss is not enough. Don't expect to hide behind a job title.

We asked Jonathan Neale, managing director of the Formula One racing team McLaren, how he established his legitimacy when he first joined the team from a completely different sector.

"It was hard," he admits. "This business works at an extraordinary pace and level of detail, and I was your archetypal big chunk thinker, so I had to come back and learn. I picked out people and spent time with them and said, okay, I'm back at school here. But what I can bring is a sense of priority, organization, and workflow management so that we can get things done better and faster. I have tried to develop with the top team a sense of what the business of racing is as a process. I stress process only as 'necessary and sufficient,' not an energy-sapping or innovatively stifling bureaucracy. Flexibility and speed must be maintained. That was something they saw as valuable."

Laura Tyson faced a similar challenge when she arrived after a period in Bill Clinton's cabinet to become dean of London Business School. She admits that she attended an early management meeting at the school and was asked by a senior member of the faculty afterward, "What is your takeaway?" to which she replied, "I have no idea." Parachuting in at the top and reading an organization is difficult. Leaders often need interpreters. Tyson found one in a professor who understood the institution, liked it, was frustrated by it, but could get things done—and then would talk to her about how he'd done it. "You must help them realize that their cleverness doesn't mean they can do other things. They may overestimate their cleverness in other areas—you must show that you are competent to help them," Tyson explains.

Surprising juxtapositions of knowledge are often the most powerful. Consider the following example. A man we'll call Tom Nelson was the marketing director of a major British brewing company—and a great example of a leader with complementary skills. Although he was not an expert on traditional brewing techniques or real ales, he was known throughout the organization as "Numbers Nelson" for his grasp of the firm's marketing performance. His fame was based on an almost uncanny ability to quote how many barrels of the company's beer were sold the day before in a given part of the country. Nelson's mastery of the firm's sales was both acknowledged and respected. He was not a brewing man, but he was demonstrably a marketing man, so the brewers took his opinions about product development seriously. For example, Nelson's reading of market tastes led to the company's development of low-alcohol beers.

Leaders with supplementary skills are perhaps more commonplace; for example, Bill Gates, when he was CEO of Microsoft, emphasized his ability as a computer programmer. Michael Critelli is chairman and former CEO of Stamford, Connecticut–based Pitney Bowes. The company, which is best known for making postage meters, holds many patents based on the research and development it carries out in new technology. The careful management of its intellectual property is important to the company's future. Critelli, a former lawyer, holds a number of patents in his own name. This gives him credibility with his clever people.

Other leaders use their own status in the clever world to get floor space. When he was chairman of GlaxoSmithKline, Richard Sykes, himself a talented scientist, insisted on being called Dr. Sykes. The title gave him respect within the professional community that his clever people belonged to in a way that being the chairman of a major multinational pharmaceutical company did not.

For others, the clever qualification is simply a bridge that allows them to communicate with their clevers in a way that they appreciate and respect. For example, Louise Makin is highly qualified (she also won the Three Peaks Race in the United Kingdom, which involves climbing Britain's highest mountains and sailing between them). "I realized that I wasn't that interested in technology per se but I was really interested in how the technology actually got to market," she says. "What having a PhD gave me was the ability to talk through a science, to interrogate scientists, to challenge scientists because if I could, I could see the thinking and follow it through. I have a sense of how their minds work. That ability to unpick a scientific argument was useful, because I could communicate with scientists and then communicate with the market."

We also know a publisher who highlights the fact that he has a PhD in all his correspondence. His authors are academics and consultants, people who take such things as serious badges of achievement. Even though his PhD is in a completely unrelated subject, the publisher believes his authors will treat him with more respect. What a leader demonstrates expertise in, and how, is crucial.

GIVE SPACE AND RESOURCES

Clever people want and need lots of resources; they are expensive to support. They need labs, libraries, equipment, specialized facilities, and all the other expensive resources they crave. Of course, you could argue that all your staff want you to win resources for themselves. What's peculiar about clever people is that they perceive their own work to be so important that it must always be well resourced. They are prone to obsession, and it is from their obsessions that organizations can generate the most value.

As one executive remarks, "You need to give them space. They need to go away and think about what it is they're trying to do. They need the space and the time to do that without getting pulled into the day-to-day requirements of running a business. If you distract them, you distract them from doing what you really want them to do. Then they get frustrated because they never get enough time to dig into it. If that happens, they probably won't complete the task, because they will know that they won't be able to do it well enough."

The issue of providing resources and space—and creating the right environment—came up time and time again in our interviews. The more astute leaders recognized that it is a fine balance between providing enough space to try out new things and creating a playground for clevers where they are not expected to deliver results.

Says ING's Neil Buckley, "The only way I and technology can be successful in this company is to give people the room to succeed. You'll always have politics around the organization, and you have to keep these people well away from politics. Most clever people— it doesn't matter what discipline they follow—are not interested in politics."

In general, we would agree, but with an important caveat. Most clevers are not interested in politics for its own sake. Their agenda is not about climbing the greasy career pole. But, and it is an important *but*, if they are not protected from the organizational "rain," clevers can and will participate in politics. Not only is this a waste of their talents; it is also highly dangerous. Because they are typically good at gaming—and because they are obsessive and take no prisoners—they can poison a culture very quickly.

Giving clever people resources and space is the only way to prevent them from using their own Machiavellian talents to extract what they need. If the leader gets this right, they establish exactly the right kind of relationship with the clever people—demonstrating the ability to facilitate performance in inevitably political contexts.

Once leaders have given them space and resources, there is rarely a need to motivate. In fact, the opposite is the case. Leaders must ensure that their clever people aren't burned out by their obsessions.

Although the conventional wisdom is that leaders should lift others through their motivational visions, we have found that clever people are frequently scornful of such attempts. It's not just that the "big picture" vision may appear to them as vacuous (although it frequently does). It's simply regarded as irrelevant to the pursuit of their obsessions. The clever creators and producers of the BBC's magnificent wildlife programs—located away from London in Bristol, in southwest England—were rarely interested in the successive "visions" of different director generals back at Broadcasting House. They simply wanted the resources and space to continue making great programs.

TELL THEM WHAT–BUT NOT HOW

While grand visions may be a distraction, a sense of direction that unifies efforts is helpful. But going beyond *what* we are doing to *how* is risky—if only because it deprives clever people of the fun of working things out for themselves. Tell them *what,* not *how.*

Craig Fields was one of the interviewees who challenged our thinking most. Leading clever people was something he, like many leaders we encountered, had really thought about—and, to be honest, his conclusions didn't always tally with our own. Yet his point of view is extremely useful and forced us to rethink many of our preconceptions.

Craig Fields has spent thirty-five years leading clever people, scientists and engineers. As he explained:

> Clever people don't need to be told—and generally don't want to be told—how to get something done. What they need is instruction on what they need to get done. It's about establishing goals and objectives rather than instructing them on how to accomplish them.
>
> Clever people are not only capable of figuring how to get something done, but they also take great pride in figuring out how to get it done *their way*, which may be better than your way. It requires a different level of instruction. If you operate at the wrong level, not only is it a waste of time, but it can actually be damaging to the relationship.

PROVIDE BOUNDARIES

Clevers need space. But they also need structure and discipline. Creating the right sort of space—sufficiently large to allow clevers to express themselves, but also with boundaries that help them focus their efforts—is vital. One without the other is dangerous and ultimately unproductive. (This topic of discipline versus freedom is one we will return to often in this book.)

As one senior executive says, "I had a guy who was working on a very big piece of analytics. He didn't have a problem with being able to do it, but he struggled to balance the priorities and day-to-day demands. It was clear we weren't making the progress. What I actually did was, I created a new responsibility for him, and I gave him more resources and clarified what we were trying to achieve. I gave him the environment that was going to enable him to succeed." This final sentence could serve as a one-line summary of the leader's job in leading clever people.

Clever people work very hard, but they need direction and protection when it is needed. "A lot of it comes down to structure. Free up the time for them, help them, understand what they need to get something done, facilitate getting it. You need to give them organized space," says one experienced executive.

GIVE PEOPLE TIME FOR QUESTIONING

An age-old instruction to children is to ask if they don't know something. This has not usually been the case with business leaders. Traditionally, exposing ignorance was akin to showing weakness. Leadership was built on knowing more—or appearing to know more. Now, however, the leadership role is more that of an informed insider, someone who is on your side but who is candid and honest about things they don't know and is not afraid to ask. A colleague once joked that the main purpose of doing a PhD is to learn that you don't know most things and you need to go and ask more knowledgeable people. It takes self-confidence to admit that you don't know something, and clever people will respect that.

So, part of the art of leading clever people is to be able and willing to ask questions—often naive questions. "Somebody's got to ask the dumb questions!" one leader joked. "When I first came in, I asked everybody the same questions and did it very deliberately," says Louise Makin. "If you ask everybody the same questions, then two things happen. You can triangulate the data and you start to get a sense of what's happening, but you also make it safe for people to give you an opinion."

Setting up situations in which questions can be asked and debates ignited is something many leaders focus on—especially at the start of their job. Every quarter, Louise Makin gathers together groups of seven or eight people. They are drawn from throughout the company. The half-day meeting is a conversation. Over time, the balance has changed. Initially, the focus was largely on complaining about the way things were. Makin admits that she struggled to understand a lot of the conversation. Now, the emphasis is on finding ways in which Makin, as CEO, and the company's other leaders can help.

Being accessible—ostentatiously so—is a means to ensure that leaders can engage and hopefully persuade clevers of the significance of shared ambitions.

One of our most persuasive interviewees was Rob Murray, CEO of the Australian brewing company Lion Nathan. A Cambridge graduate and then a high flier with global giant Nestlé, Murray is clever and persuasively forthright. Dressed casually and sitting alongside a colleague in his impressive central Sydney offices, he observed, "Some people in the business avoid dialog and engagement with them [the clevers], because they feel intellectually intimidated. So the number one rule is, even if you realize as a CEO you're talking to people who are academically more astute than you are, you've got to be prepared to go in there and be prepared to engage them. You've got to be prepared to explain why it's really important to you to engage them effectively and what it is you're trying to achieve."

Murray continues, "They tend to admire that intellectual engagement, some would say confrontation. I think it's really important to find out what success looks like for them, because my experience is, they tend to define success themselves. They're incredibly well informed. They often have great confidence about their own capacity to earn money if they need it. They tend to see the world through their own eyes. They can get all the information they want, whenever they want to. Material wealth isn't a great concern. And success for them often is not what you would suspect it is."

The obvious can be difficult. Giving people time to air their concerns, worries, and aspirations sounds straightforward. But the time of the leader is limited, and clever people tend to prefer different communication channels. One size does not fit all.

What was interesting in talking to leaders was that all had experimented with different communication formats.

"I had to walk around and give them face time. They had to know that I knew what they were doing. But I didn't have to give them any feedback on how they were doing all that often," says Alison Fields of her experience working with IT professionals.

What's more, it's important that being accessible does not look like interference. Notes Craig Fields, "Bad managers of clever people pull the flower out of the ground daily to be sure that the roots are healthy—checking and rechecking clever people is not appreciated," he observes. The task of the clever leader is to understand and engage their followers—not to be seen as limiting their precious freedoms. Leave the flowers in the ground and let them grow. And when they do grow, it is important to recognize the gardener. This brings us to the next point.

GIVE RECOGNITION AND AMPLIFY ACHIEVEMENTS

What clever people do is central to their identity—so recognizing their achievements is vital. This is why movie credits seem to become ever longer. They recognize the contribution of each and every person, from the star to the best boy. Seeing your name—however small the font and empty the movie house—is important.

Yet many clever people are starved of recognition within their own organizations. Although they may want it personally, they are rarely sufficiently concerned with the need to deliver it to their immediate colleagues.

Alison Fields comments, "One person was practically in tears when I wrote his performance appraisal, because no one had ever appreciated what he had done before. Another person gave a briefing, and as we were walking out, I said that was a really good briefing. I wasn't even thinking about it other than he had done a really good briefing. He was a very senior person, and he said that in the last ten years none of his bosses had ever complimented him on anything."

For recognition to be effective, much turns on the *type* of recognition that is delivered, *from whom,* and *how often.* Regular praise from a manager (a suit) who is widely regarded as a jerk is unlikely to be motivating. An industry award every few years or a single paper highly cited by valued peers may be far more rewarding. Clever people tend to value recognition from prestigious peers and clients outside their organizations the most.

What's more—given their sensitivities to interference and the fact that many may be working on long and complex tasks with unknowable outcomes—although recognition is highly valued, it does not necessarily need to be delivered frequently. Quality, not quantity.

As Fields reveals, with intermittent recognition it is particularly important to get it right. Recognition comes in a huge and imaginative variety of forms. It need not be rocket science even if the person you are recognizing is a rocket scientist. Nestlé introduced a public open day at its research center in Lausanne, Switzerland. There was an exhibition making a link between the R&D work done at the center and everyday products. The people who worked at the center brought their families and friends and exuded pride as they showed them how science was translated into complete products, and quality and taste, and so on.

Recognition can be simply a matter of joining a team when the members have an end-of-week or end-of-project beer. "I spent a lot of time going out to pubs with programmers at the end of a project," one leader told us. "That was a kind of recognition that seemed to work much more than giving them some sort of bureaucratic award or something. But everybody going out to the pub together and having the boss there; I didn't stay all that long so they could have more fun after I left."

A surgeon told of us a change in his working arrangements, with widespread repercussions. It wasn't the budget-conscious refusal of the hospital to invest in more new technology. Nor was it staff cuts. Instead, the hospital managers decided that surgeons should no longer be provided with free sandwiches at lunchtime. After all, it cost money, and no other group in the hospital was provided with free food. After spending hours saving people's lives, the surgeons now go to the canteen like everyone else.

Of course, in the cause of fairness, this was the right decision. What it overlooked was that the sandwiches had become symbolic tokens of recognition from the hospital to its surgical stars. The fact that even mundane sandwiches can be seen as symbols of recognition by highly paid men and women with brilliant careers demonstrates just how difficult (and also how simple) recognition can be.

ENCOURAGE FAILURE, MAXIMIZE LEARNING

Some clever people, particularly in specialist or expert roles, may become data driven and risk averse. "Help make our market researchers more entrepreneurial!" was the cry we heard from senior executives tired of their colleagues' painful paralysis "because they never have enough information." The challenge for the leaders was to make specialists more comfortable with risk taking.

But in many contexts the problem is the reverse. It's about helping clever people deal with the consequences of risk—failure—in a way in which they will learn.

Any organization that strives for high levels of innovation and creativity—exactly the area where clever people make a big difference—must recognize the necessity of failure. In pushing the frontiers of knowledge, clever people live on the perennial edge of failure. Better that than mediocrity or passive acceptance of the status quo. Not all innovations can work. For every successful new pharmaceutical product, there are dozens of failures; for every hit record, hundreds of duds. The leader of clever people must recognize this, acknowledge it to followers, but at the same time, distinguish between the inevitability of failure associated with innovation and straightforward error. The former may even require celebration, while the latter stimulates a whole range of coaching, feedback, and even confrontation techniques more normally associated with performance management.

Consider a pharmaceuticals example, involving Glaxo. When three high-tech antibiotics in the final stages of clinical trials all failed, Richard Sykes, then chairman, responded by sending letters of congratulation to the team leaders thanking them for killing the drugs and encouraging them to move on to the next challenge. This is inspired leadership of clever people.

Whereas many organizations need to train people intensively in order to reduce risks of failure, clever people often arrive highly trained in professional or technical terms. Paradoxically, they may get cleverer mainly by organizations maximizing opportunities for failure. This is because they tend to respond best to difficult, stretching tasks where their talents are tested to the limits. By contrast, their attitude toward "training events" (particularly managerially inspired) can be scornful.

We worked with the top team at a large law firm where the major challenge was to get the team to learn but not through training. They viewed conventional training with disdain and as interference with their fee-billing activities. They learned best when faced with the next difficult assignment with an important client. This is learning the hard way—but clever people appear particularly drawn to it. They may not always like it, but learn they must.

PROTECT CLEVER PEOPLE FROM THE RAIN

Clever people see the administrative machinery of the organization as a distraction from their key value-adding activities. So they need to be protected from the organizational "rain." "I manage people 24/7," says Julie McEver at New Philanthropy Capital. "It's when I ease their pressure, I get them the resources. When I clear up their time to focus, they know I'll do that again. It's my role to figure out the organization."

The leader sweeps aside the organizational detritus. Leading clevers is all about removing obstacles that prevent them doing what they do best. Sometimes, that means knocking down the barriers; other times it means keeping the red tape at bay.

"I think you've got a responsibility to protect people from as much crap as is possible. I mean, what do we want from our cardiac surgeons? Primarily, we want them to be churning out excellence, and moving the agenda forward, in the management of patients, in cardiac surgery. We don't want them filling out pieces of paper," says neurosurgeon Peter Lees with characteristic common sense.

Adds Fujitsu's Marc Silvester, "First and foremost, it's my job to manage our management and to set the conditions and the environment for our people to be successful. That's what I get paid to do. I'd love to do the work they are doing, which is why I want to set it up so that they can get it done. But it's my job to set up the relationships and to guard the playground, if you like. Stop the things coming up behind and overwhelming the young kids with new ideas who have just arrived for the new term. All the older kids are running around because they know how things have been done in the past, and have great confidence in this. So it's my job to protect the new, their ability to get it done, and promote the conditions and the enjoyment of having got it done."

Since clever people are organizationally savvy (but not necessarily motivated to engage in extensive politicking), they are often aware of the protection that leaders may be offering them. In fact, the most skillful leaders *ensure* that they know this. In effect, they build up credit with their grateful followers, who in turn realize they must reciprocate favors.

GIVE REAL-WORLD CHALLENGES WITH CONSTRAINTS

It is sometimes suggested that individuals can be energized to achieve goals by leaders encouraging them to believe that everything is possible. But this kind of optimism is not always successful with clever people. Their preference seems to be the reverse. Tell them something is not possible, and they will be highly motivated to prove you wrong. Says Marc Silvester, "The best challenges are those where people tell you that you can't do something. You find the money and the people and get it done. That is my style."

This is in stark contrast to the old prevailing orthodoxy. This asserted that you got the best from clever people by freeing them from constraint in some delicious setting as far away from the real world as possible: a kind of organizational ivory tower.

Craig Fields recounts:

The way to get the best output was to have small teams of people, and give them what I call difficult challenges. And challenges with constraints. How can you get this done within a month? How can you get this done within a million dollars? And that, I always found, produced the most directed burst of energy. So a challenge to achieve particular output is what gets the juices flowing of clever people.

I had a group, and we were talking about building a super-computer. I said, let's build a supercomputer, a trillion float-ing point operations per second—at that time, years ago, a seemingly impossible challenge. They looked at me as if I was crazy. It was as if I asked them to get to the moon by jumping. It was absolutely inconceivable and impossible. I kept pressing them and giving them examples of how we might approach it. And after a while people got on board with this as a great goal and did it.

Clever people are at their most productive when faced with real and hard questions that they must solve within meaningful con-straints. This is how EA's Will Wright puts it: "If you go up to these guys and say, 'I wish we could do this, but I don't think it's possi-ble!' this is by far and away the best way to motivate them. If I go past and say, 'I wish we could do this, but I don't think we can do that, so we're going to have to do this boring thing instead,' in every case, if the programmer is up to the task, it's the best way to motivate them. They will spend every waking hour saying, 'I bet there is a way to solve it—I know there is a way.' They really enjoy it. It's like the thrill of the hunt."

TALK STRAIGHT

Earlier, we described the humility of the effective leaders we had encountered during our research. We made the point then that this is not about being soft with clevers: indeed, often the leaders demonstrated steely will. This points to another aspect of the role. In order to flourish, leaders must be confident about their own expertise. If they are not, the clevers will sense it. They have good antennae for bull. To be an effective leader of clevers, you have to know who you are—and be confident in your own abilities. (In our previous book, we advised leaders to "be yourself—more—with skill." When you're leading clevers, that applies in spades!)

One of our interviewees was Joe Woolf. He first visited Vietnam at the beginning of the 1990s when he was posted to Ho Chi Minh City to run an oil exploration operation. Now he is founder of Atlas Industries, with offices in London, Sydney, and Dubai, that uses Vietnamese architects. We asked Woolf how, as a nonarchitect, he went about establishing credibility with his teams of architects.

His answer was both refreshingly direct and unflinching. "I've got glass walls in my office, and I can see two hundred people all doing jobs which I couldn't do, and I'm very happy to acknowledge that," he told us. "I also tell them, if anybody wants to do my job and can, they're welcome to it. Good luck."

This sort of confidence is vital. Leading clever people requires that the leader be in touch with how they add value and how their skills complement those of the people they lead.

Another leader told us about how he dealt with someone who got into a bad-tempered disagreement with a client. "I told him to go back and apologize. That was one of the few times I actually had to order someone to do something. I finally got him to do it, and he came back and he said, 'My god, I now have the moral high ground. They're so upset that I apologized, and they said now they're feeling that they're in the wrong.' I said, 'Well, they are, but you shouldn't have done it.' And he said, 'I understand now.'"

Explaining and persuading requires that communication lines must always be open and two-way. If you tell people what's going on, they might return the compliment. Sir Graeme Davies has spent his career in academia, first as an academic, then as a leader of academics. He now leads the University of London. "My experience of clever people is, they will live with anything, disaster, difficulty, providing they know what is going on. If they think backdoor deals are being done, you're done for," he says.

Adds Louise Makin, "The skill with clever people is openness. I need to know bad news, good news, hopes and fears, what might happen, because there's a tendency to think you can't bring the CEO bad news." Indeed, leaders can become isolated from reality, insulated from the humdrum.

Transparency rules also because clever people have a low tolerance for bull.. Their typically uneasy relationship with organizations makes them supersensitive to perceived deceit, corporatespeak, double-dealing, or any other strategy that implies they can be easily duped.

CREATE A GALAXY

Clever people require a peer group of like-minded individuals. This means that leaders must be highly selective about who they recruit. Universities have long understood this. Hire a star professor, and you can be sure the young aspiring PhDs in that subject will flock to your institution. They want to work with and be inspired by someone they admire. The same magnet effect works in investment banking (think of Goldman Sachs) and creative industries.

Attracting the right clever people is an increasingly recognized and important task for leaders. As ING's Neil Buckley pointed out, when you start looking from an IT perspective, there's the predictable, discipline side, which is about keeping it running, and then there's the enablement and the differentiating side, which is with your creative, clever, and driven people. Says Buckley:

> In IT you can split the two 40/60. You've got 60 running the place, 40 doing the changes. Now, out of that 40, you're only

looking at maybe four or five people who are your real creative, clever people. It's a very small number. What happens with creative people is, people, who want to be like them see themselves in their light but don't have their ability, align themselves with them. You need to be able to tap that motivational skill. Particularly with junior people, young graduates, if you can get those real thought leaders and riders, keep them motivated and on a path, they can pull your organization with it. If you don't enable them, they can destroy the organization; so it is a very fine balance, but it is really a question of identifying them.

Great people are always great hires. Kamlesh Pande observes that "in India, clever people assume the role of catalysts and role models. In many cases, this happens unknowingly. When, in an organization, five people become catalysts and role models, the impact on the rest is huge. There is no point in having only pockets of excellence in an organization; it has to go to the grass roots."

All of these interviewees, in their different ways, illustrate the same fundamental point. While it is conventional wisdom to seek to attract stars to an organization, the real leadership task is to ensure that these stars are connected to each other in ways that influence the entire organization. The leader is building a social architecture of knowledge. It's akin to using the best players on your soccer team to set the standards for everyone.

CONDUCT AND CONNECT

As we have said throughout this chapter, many of those we interviewed had struggled hard with trying to understand and elucidate exactly what they did in a leadership role. Indeed, just as clever people say they don't want to be led, so many say they do not wish to see themselves as "leaders"—at least as this role is often conventionally understood.

Those leaders who had really thought about their roles often sought out metaphors to explain what they did:

The leader as compass. Werner Bauer: "If you don't give them the main axis, they get very confused. They need the compass, and this is your role really, to give that compass, that direction, whether it's north or south."

The leader as magnet. Louise Makin: "You have to be a magnetic field. You never touch anything."

The leader as bridge. Marc Silvester: "In an organization like this, and in this industry, you will find people going either towards the technical side, or they will go towards general management. There is a massive gap, both in people resource terms and also in intellectual connection terms, between those two camps. So my role is bridging those two camps."

The live leader. Rob Murray: "Via a combination of bosses, peers, PAs, or even direct reports, you must connect clever people to the rest of the business. My analogy would be that many appliances, but not all, still need plugs in order to connect with the power supply. Sometimes this connection is the practical stuff—e.g., personal organization and knowledge of 'how to get things done through others'—but often it's the humanistic ability to empathize and see the world from others' points of view; many clever people have a blind spot here born of their own conviction that their way is definitely the right way."

So, we have a compass, a magnetic field, a bridge, and a plug. Leading clevers is hard. It's even harder to describe. But we have learned a lot from our respondents. They have made us reconsider some of our most cherished assumptions about organizations— deliberately so, for we may need to reconsider some of our most cherished assumptions about organizations.

Remember, there is a paradox at work here. Clevers challenge several aspects of the traditional working relationship. First, they don't want to be led, but they need leadership to achieve their potential and create value for society. Second, they enjoy a symbiotic relationship with the organization. In the past, individuals were expected to add value to the organization; but in the clever economy, the organization and its leaders must ask themselves how they can add value to their clever individuals.

The fundamental issue underpinning all of this is how clevers connect with each other and with the organization. That is the main theme of the next part of the book. In it, we examine what happens when clever people work together.

PART TWO

CLEVER TEAMS

3 THE ANATOMY OF CLEVER TEAMS

MILLIONS OF WORDS have been written about the war for talent in the business world. While we agree that star performers are in short supply and can make a big difference in whether an organization thrives or dives, we take issue with one aspect of the coverage. Much of it has focused on the individual. So, for example, when a top fund manager is poached by a rival investment bank, it makes the business headlines. But what is often underplayed is that they are taking their team with them. This is an important point. Why? Well, we believe that clever people make their biggest contribution when they work as part of a team.

Few organizations symbolize the clever economy better than the United Kingdom–based Formula One auto-racing team McLaren. This is where cleverness meets the alluring sexiness of speed. Founded in 1963 by New Zealander Bruce McLaren (1937–1970) initially as a builder of sports cars, McLaren today is best known as a Formula One constructor but has also competed in the Indianapolis 500-Mile Race and the Canadian-American Challenge Cup.

McLaren is one of the most successful teams in Formula One, having won over 150 races, 11 Drivers' Championships, and 8 Constructors' Championships. At the time of writing, McLaren's Lewis Hamilton, just twenty-three years old and one of the most exciting young drivers to emerge in recent years, had just won the Drivers' Championship in 2008, having come within a whisker of winning the title in 2007, his rookie year.

According to industry insiders, McLaren has technical resources that are more sophisticated than any other team and a resulting higher development rate through the season.

At McLaren Racing's sci-fi-like headquarters, set somewhat incongruously in the leafy commuter heartland of southern England, we talked with Jonathan Neale. He joined McLaren as operations director in 2001, taking on responsibility for manufacturing, supply chain, transport and logistics, and purchasing. Since 2004, he has been managing director, running the engineering departments, and more involved in technical strategy and direction.

Part of Jonathan Neale's drive at McLaren is to bring more operational productivity and excellence to its activities. "Five or six years ago, we were trying to get the technical organization to accept targets," he recalls. "If you're going to invest tens of millions of dollars in a new car, it's a good idea to have some sense that it's going to be better than the old one and better than the competition's. But the engineers could not, at that stage, reconcile in their minds the sense of absoluteness about the target. (Well, I don't know what I'm competing against, so how can I possibly set a target?) How do I know my car's going to be quicker than a Ferrari or a Renault? Well, the answer is, you don't, but we believe you have to aim at something. A simple example was the certainty that if we launch the new car with an engine next year that develops 500 brake horsepower, we would probably be at the back of the grid, but I know if we go with 900 brake horsepower, we will be likely to blow them into the weeds."

Neale admits to being surprised initially by the reticence of the McLaren engineers to accept such measures. On reflection, however, given the nature of precision and rigor in the engineering development process, it is easy to see how finite target setting could be at odds with the excellence objective. After all, how good is "good enough" in a product-excellence business? Over time, however, there has been growing acceptance of the benefits of being target driven. "Part of the reticence was fear of the consequence of missing a target. The answer is, we'll learn from it," he says.

Previously, Neale worked in the aerospace industry, where development programs typically took fifteen years and late delivery was regrettably commonplace. In Formula One, he points out, delivery is nonnegotiable. It has to be spectacularly on time every time; the race will start with or without you when the five red lights go out. In a pit stop, McLaren has twenty-seven people with approximately 7 seconds to change all the wheels and refuel. Teams have been scrambled on the Friday afternoon before a Sunday race to sort out a problem. Neale has more than once chartered a plane to ensure that a particular part arrives on time. "We have one thousand people on the programme whose single objective is to win. You just cannot be fifteen minutes late for a Grand Prix. The Monaco Grand Prix racing car has to be available on Friday morning, not the next race or the race afterwards; it's then. There's a tremendous sense of against all odds we made it happen—and that's not infrequent. So, there is something about that immediacy, the constant nature of change, which gives us lots of opportunities to learn."

McLaren has around 140 engineers. Jonathan Neale describes them this way:

They are very bright, highly loaded with IQ and hardwired for logic, not particularly emotional, but to a man, they dislike being managed. Management is a term that is, I wouldn't say derisive, but a necessary evil. Somebody's got to do it because it's the way things work, but don't get in my way. Management's got to be seen to add value by helping, not hindering.

We've stayed true to having very bright, technically gifted people staying close to the product at the top of the organization. I think once organizations become large, there is a tendency to promote management skills as you come through engineering, and that tends to promote a level of bureaucracy, and ultimately engineering directors that become little more than engineering resource managers or figureheads, but don't actually know the product or inspire the younger engineers. We expect managers to lead and inspire by being in the trenches with the troops. Young engineers will work incredibly hard here. Yes, it's a sexy product. Yes, there is a pass or fail test every two weeks. And it's a good business to be in. But what we expect of them is demanding and sometimes arduous.

With incredibly tight timescales, there is no room for egos to get in the way. The emphasis is on moving more quickly and sharing information. "People need room to operate. They need a proper job to get their teeth into, they need to be challenged. We move towards problems. We don't ignore things," is how Jonathan Neale describes the McLaren approach.

On race weekends, Neale does not have an operational role. It is down to the driver, the engineers and the mechanics. But, of course, he's there, keeping his eyes and ears open, and watching. Watching how people are, what they're like under pressure, and what works and what doesn't. "What I'd like to do is leave a winning chapter in the book of McLaren," he says. "It's all about winning, winning. So, if that's what it's about, that's what we've got to be committed to. In the last ten laps of the race, you'll find me in the garage, pacing up and down and looking for Prozac!"

Back at McLaren headquarters in Woking, Neale walks around, sensing this situation. He is particularly on the lookout for what he calls "long thin projects." He explains:

Things get started for all the right reasons, and then somebody becomes attached to the principle or somebody becomes ingrained with wanting to make sure this works, and you think, hang on, this has been running for six weeks and we're not seeing the results. Then quickly [the projects] have to be killed off and moved on to something else. We have an excellence business model and can-do attitude. As a consequence, when some projects run on for too long or lose focus, people are sometimes unwilling to admit defeat or give up and move on to a more lap-time productive task. And part of my job is to go round and shoot poor projects. It's like pruning.

It is a tough business. Neale cites his experience on the factory floors of Manchester and Ayrshire as formative and still useful. For all the wonderful aesthetics, soft furnishings, and the sheer sexiness of speed, McLaren's is not a cozy world. Engineers are never short of an opinion. "I like it to be honest," says Jonathan Neale. "Whatever we're doing, we're going with positive intent. There's a strong sense of squad and a desire for it to be Fortress McLaren. If we are going to learn we have to be frank about what is really going on. Whatever the problem is, we have to be flexible, adaptive, and quick. We always strive to take decisions at the point of most knowledge. I don't have most knowledge. I have a lot of authority, but I use that authority to set standards, enable, weed out, prune, set direction, and agree change. I don't use that authority to dictate what must be done."

In the clever team world of Formula One, leadership is a subtle combination of discipline and distance, rigor and restlessness, thoughtful speed.

NICHE

From fast cars to high finance—everywhere we looked, we found that clever teams are the differentiator. Consider Goldman Sachs, one of the few investment banks to come out of the subprime debacle with its reputation intact. It, of course, has individual bankers with staggeringly large remuneration deals. But the bank's culture is suspicious of star players, and it does all it can to prevent deal makers from becoming maverick individuals. When they think creatively in pursuit of money-making opportunities, even the most high-performing individuals are urged to talk their ideas through with the team—in particular, the risk managers who see it as their job to protect the firm's reputation.

At McLaren, Goldman Sachs, and other clever organizations, the team is the thing. There are exceptions, of course, but most of the examples we have researched turn out to be team based—even if one individual gets most of the credit. Think about Lewis Hamilton at McLaren, for instance. Is he a very talented racing driver? Yes, of course. To challenge for the Formula One World Championship in his first season, as he did in 2007, and then to win it in his second season, he would have to be. But did he do it all on his own? No, of course not; Hamilton is a product of McLaren's Young Driver Program, which helped hone his skills from the age of twelve. To compete in Formula One, he also relied on an amazingly talented group of engineers, mechanics, and others. Together, they form a clever team—or, perhaps, several clever teams.

The yachtsman and adventurer Pete Goss is another powerful example. He is perhaps best known for his heroic rescue—in the teeth of a hurricane—of a French competitor in the Vendée Globe single-handed round-the-world yacht race. For this, Goss was awarded the *Legion d'Honneur,* France's highest award for gallantry. He has also been awarded an MBE (Member of the British Empire) and been named Yachtsman of the Year. Goss has a string of other achievements to his name, including the development of a revolutionary catamaran sponsored by Team Philips.

There is no doubt that Goss is a big character—driven by a fierce personal passion and a determination to succeed. But he is not the larger-than-life figure that you might expect. Meet him face-to-face, and you will encounter a modest, self-effacing, and—by his own admission—shy man. Above all, he will remind you that a "single-handed" yacht race is a misnomer—that all his achievements have been built upon the efforts of a "very large family" whose complementary strengths are what eventually produce success.

Or think of a brain surgeon like Peter Lees. He comes from a family of three generations of doctors. He is a neurosurgeon but, since the 1980s, has been one of the champions of leadership in the United Kingdom's National Health Service. Lees's faith in leadership is powerfully straightforward. "Leadership saves lives," he says. Lees is now medical director and director of leadership at the NHS South Central Strategic Health Authority. He is resolutely—and reassuringly—down-to-earth about his own surgical skills and emphasizes the role of the wider team. "What we're very bad at in the public sector is connecting everybody with the success of something—in our case, treating patients." Patients get better through teamwork.

Show us a clever person who is making a real difference to their organization, and we'll show you a clever team behind them.

PAINTING BY TEAM NUMBERS

Today, as innovation becomes ever more vital to competitiveness, the team has moved to center stage. More and more work in the knowledge economy is done in teams because the complexity of the work demands it. Indeed, as workplaces and organizations have changed, so, too, has our understanding of what a team means.

Since the 1970s, the notion of teamwork has been transformed. As companies recognized the growing importance of innovation, so they acknowledged the need to harness collaboration among their people. This changed the meaning of teamwork. Rewind just forty years, for instance, and teamwork was largely about compliance: doing as you were told, following instructions from your manager, and avoiding conflict. Then, in the 1970s, it became focused on small, face-to-face teams working collaboratively rather than merely implementing orders from a boss. Think of the growing influence of the Japanese-inspired practices of Total Quality Management and *kaizen*, or continuous improvement, which relied on teams of workers who were prepared to constantly seek ways of improving processes. In the last decade, the notion of teamwork has further evolved, to cover complex processes spanning many different parts of the organization, geographic locations, and indeed multiple firms.

So, clever teams come in many shapes and sizes. They range from the leader and his or her direct reports to—increasingly—cross-functional teams, task forces, and ad hoc problem-focused teams. Some leaders find their teams strung along the corridor beside them. Others—again increasingly—find themselves running geographically dispersed teams spread across every continent.

Louise Makin at BTG plc has a development team that includes life scientists who are working with chemists outside the company, as well as with small companies that provide expertise in chemistry, manufacturing, clinical trials, and management. "The very first thing they're doing is working in concert, and this is critical to us," she explains. "We have to manage clever people as an integrated set because no one person in this company can make a call about a program because it's about the drug. It's about the medical need. It's about the market need. It's about the regulatory pathway. It's about the IP [intellectual property]. So, actually, I need four or five people to come together. Each of them is really clever and knows their area, but actually just adding those up isn't enough."

None of this is straightforward. Bringing people together rarely is. "If I need to have more than three or four clever people in one team, which is of tremendous importance and value to the organization, then I need to be really good at conflict management. Because three clever people will never think alike. They will pull themselves apart, and it is my role to make sure that I find a common goal for them," observes Kamlesh Pande.

"Clever teams really, really challenge you. You can't motivate them," concedes Louise Makin. "In my previous job I used performance management. Why are we here? What are we doing? Now I think of the phrase *expectation management*. I paint the picture of what I want or what we all want, and we paint it together and we get excited about what it could look like. People will step forward for themselves. You can't make them step forward. It's how you create an expectation of what you want, and it's also about the feel of the thing and what it means for everybody when we're successful."

SHOCKLEY AND AWE

Yet despite their potential, talent-rich teams are not all world-conquering, problem-solving, record-breaking triumphs. Truth be told: clever teams regularly screw up. Some of the difficulties raised in leading clever teams can be seen in the salutary tale of William Shockley.[1]

Shockley was a British-born research scientist who worked at the Bell Laboratories during the postwar period developing the transistor. In 1947 Shockley was recognized as the coinventor of the transistor, and in 1956 he was awarded a Nobel Prize. In 1955, he left the Bell Labs to found his own company, Shockley Semiconductor Laboratory, situated in Palo Alto, California. His academic reputation attracted some of the finest minds in electronics to his company. These included Robert Noyce and Gordon Moore (of Moore's Law fame), who went on to cofound Intel.

Shockley was blessed with a brilliant mind. He was described by Bob Noyce as a "marvelous intuitive problem solver" and by Gordon Moore as having "phenomenal physical intuition." But unfortunately for Shockley, his leadership skills fell far short of his intellectual brilliance.

On one occasion, Shockley asked some of his younger employees what he could do to help enthuse them. Several expressed a wish to publish research papers. So Shockley went home, wrote a paper, and returned the next day, offering to let them publish the paper in their own names. Well meant but not well led.

In another example, Shockley instituted a secret "project within a project" at the company. Although only fifty or so people were working at Shockley Labs, when some of the group were employed to work on Shockley's new idea—which, according to Shockley, had the potential to rival that of the transistor—they were not allowed to discuss the project with other colleagues. It wasn't long before rumblings of discontent with Shockley's leadership style were fanned into the flames of mutiny.

The situation deteriorated and a disenchanted group left to found Fairchild Semiconductor in 1957. The company went on to revolutionize the world of computing through its work on the silicon transistor. Just as importantly, it spun off a slew of talent who went on to start up some of the best-known companies in Silicon Valley. Intel (Bob Noyce and Gordon Moore), Advanced Micro Devices (Jerry Sanders), and National Semiconductor (Charlie Sporck) were all spin-offs from Fairchild.

Shockley's poor leadership of clever people inadvertently laid the cornerstone of Silicon Valley. First, he had brought together a group of the best scientists in the field of electronics, many of whom might not have otherwise remained in the San Francisco area. Second, he had created the conditions necessary to provoke his brilliant employees to leave and start up on their own.

APOLLO LANDING

The points above underline our observation that simply putting clever people together does not make them a team. There are many examples of extremely bright and talented groups that signally underperform. We have seen this phenomenon many times in the course of our research: a company cherry-picks its cleverest people, removes the day-to-day responsibilities of their jobs, and heaps resources—equipment, time, and money—on them. Having lighted the clever fuse in this way, the organization retreats to a safe distance to watch the innovative pyrotechnics. Often, though, the result is a hugely expensive and ultimately frustrating dud. This should not come as any great surprise.

The fallibility of apparently clever teams is not a new discovery. Meredith Belbin carried out groundbreaking work on team working in the late 1960s and early 1970s.[2] One of Belbin's earliest discoveries about clever people (although he didn't use the term) led him to theorize about the ideal composition of teams. He called it the Apollo Syndrome. What Belbin noticed was that high-IQ individuals frequently performed badly when they were put together in a team. In competitive situations, Belbin found that teams consisting of less clever people typically outperformed teams of clever people.

Our own observations confirm this. Several of McLaren's competitors have put together over the past 10 years star-studded teams that to-date have underperformed. We have repeatedly encountered groups of very clever individuals who fail to perform as a team. The challenge in the clever economy is to develop teams of clever individuals who can perform collectively.

CARING AND SHARING

So let's go back to basics. What is a team? The simplest definition that distinguishes a team is that there are shared objectives; there are interdependent tasks; and members are aware of each other's existence.

It sounds simple, doesn't it? But we have regularly observed clever people struggling with these basics and so failing as a team. Let's take the elements in turn.

SHARED OBJECTIVES

We opened with the imperative of teamwork at McLaren. But it should be remembered that Lewis Hamilton's dramatic first season was marred by regular stories about his problematic relationship with McLaren's resident "star" driver, Fernando Alonso. The upstart rookie started the season as the team's number two driver. Soon he was pushing the senior and number one driver aside—usually at high speed. Clearly, these individual tensions threatened the team—as they may in many star-driven cultures. Think, for example, of the entertainment industry or financial services. Many rock bands have been riven by an inability to work together. Indeed, the exceptions, like the Four Tops, the Rolling Stones, or U2, are noticeable by their rarity. *Artistic differences* is a euphemism for a failure in team working.

Shared objectives are also threatened where the focus is more on external relations with personal clients than with each other in a team. We worked with the top team of a law firm where the primary focus of senior partners was on maximizing revenues (and personal income) through building client business in their separate specialties or geographies. This is not unusual in many professional firms. Top team meetings designed to build a sense of shared strategic purpose were seen as a distraction. Meetings were regularly interrupted by individual partners taking client calls or dealing with client-driven emergencies—often to the fury of the managing partner. Attempts to build shared goals were tolerated but rarely taken seriously once people were outside the meeting and back to business—where, in effect, partners vigorously pursued their own goals.

Witness also the struggles of several investment banks to produce a "one firm" mentality that links together private banking, investment banking, and asset management to better service individual clients seamlessly. Many have failed. Credit Suisse—through its Project Uno strategy—has been cleverly attempting to reintegrate its investment bank, Credit Suisse First Boston. It has thought of new ways to reward cooperation, launched a new logo, and appointed an American investment banker as its new Zurich-based CEO. It is still a work in progress, but the company seems to be ahead of its rivals.

Differing professional norms and work orientations also undermine shared goals. Think back to Peter Lees and his leadership challenges at the NHS. Teams of skillful, dedicated, and highly talented individuals in most health services in most parts of the world are regularly pulled apart by contrasting agendas. The consultant concerned with high professional standards—and the status that accompanies it; the nurse focused on daily patient care; the administrator determined to deliver efficient services; and the many different, but interdependent, teams across specialist units, hospitals, and regions—fighting for the same scarce resources. When we spoke with NHS CEO David Nicholson, he pithily observed, "The culture is built around individuals—this can get tricky when there are thousands of them."

INTERDEPENDENCE

This leads us to the second issue: interdependence. Let's not pretend—many clever "teams" are just not teams at all according to this criterion. Several top teams that we have worked with, for example, are essentially groups of representatives with no real interdependencies. When they come together, it's primarily to exchange information, update each other on some routine metrics, and perhaps agree on or amend some common binding norms or standards. Rarely—if ever—do they work together interdependently as a team on a shared task. Quite the reverse: they often spend a fair part of their meetings protecting their turf. Up to a point, we have no problems with this; but it might make sense (and relieve a fair amount of angst) if these "teams" dropped the pretense.

Where there are real—or potential—interdependencies, these can be threatened by the strong drive of clever people to retain their autonomy and independence. We have witnessed this regularly with our faculty colleagues, who will often resist, for example, a rational case for smaller departments to merge, in order to protect their own intellectual freedoms. But remember, as Louise

Makin and Jonathan Neale make clear, there are often pressing work-related needs that mean that clever individuals have to co-operate. It is hard to imagine that a new pharmaceutical product can be developed at Roche, Novartis, or Novo Nordisk without embracing the challenge of complex interdependencies—among the various disciplines of R&D and among R&D, sales and marketing, and manufacturing.

AWARENESS OF OTHERS' EXISTENCE

This may seem to be the most basic requirement—yet it frequently proves to be the undoing of clever teams. Even where an individual is physically surrounded by other members of the team, that person sometimes appears not to see them. Think of the infuriating behavior of the star soccer striker who regularly goes for the goal, when two other players are clearly better placed to score if only they received the pass. If eighty thousand fans can see the other players, why can't he?

But if this kind of behavior is simple selfishness, other instances may be more generously explained by the nature of clever work and of clever teams. Some clever work is characterized by very low levels of interaction, for example. A university professor may just not spend enough time with a fellow member of the faculty to realize that she contributes to the same program and provides inputs that overlap with his own. Similarly, a member of a large, complex global research team may simply be unaware of its shifting membership. Although this may sound extraordinary, remember that many clevers—in pharmaceuticals or IT, for example—hold multiple memberships on teams within highly complex, matrixed structures. It appears that too regularly the designers of clever teams forget a basic maxim: identification increases with interaction.

Finally, some clever work is completely engrossing. Those who do it become lost in the task, losing touch with others and the world. Here is one senior executive and consultant, quoted in

Paul Glen's book *Leading Geeks*, reflecting on the work of the IT specialist:

> "One of the great joys of geekwork is that it is fundamentally creative. It requires losing oneself in a problem, focusing thoughts on a small piece of reality, and staying with it for long periods of time. You can't create software or design hardware while thinking about your bank account, your car, or what your children will eat for dinner. The minutiae of everyday life melt away as you focus on only the problem at hand . . . If a geek gets interrupted while trying to concentrate on technical work, it's a long journey back to reality."[3]

We encountered many clevers (often sources of great value) who were so obsessed with their work that they seemed utterly unaware of the organizational context. Indeed, as long as the organization continued to fund their obsessions, they didn't really care who they worked for.

But when clever teams get this right—shared goals, interdependence, and awareness of each other's existence—the results can be literally life changing. Peter Donnelly, chairman of the Wellcome Trust Case Control Consortium and a professor of statistical science at Oxford University, told us how producing cooperation among about two hundred scientists working on twenty-five different projects took us much closer to understanding the link between human genetics and the predisposition to diseases. More than twenty genes predisposing people to ailments such as heart disease and diabetes were discovered by analyzing five hundred thousand genetic variants from each of seventeen thousand volunteers. What was amazing was that this research involved researchers, usually dedicated to no-holds-barred competition, actually working constructively together. The different teams were largely self-managing, with a central management committee linked by regular conference calls. The lure for the researchers was the chance to work with a huge sample and the economies of scale that this offered.[4]

THE IDEOLOGY OF CLEVER TEAMS

So, clevers in teams may struggle with the basics of team working. A further wrinkle is that the shape, character, and contexts of these teams vary. Those we encountered at Arup—the world-renowned consulting engineers—and at McLaren, for example, were both dominated by clever engineers, but their experiences in teams were quite different, for a variety of reasons. History, tradition, and culture play a part. So, too, do goals, technology, and timescales. The nature of the products, the competitive environment, the interests of customers—all these factors are likely to influence the performance challenges of clever teams and the leadership required.

The result is that clever teams come in a variety of guises within organizations. The range we describe here draws to a large extent on how clever people see themselves: as techies, creatives, problem solvers, professionals, strategists, or even senior managers. Each may have its own ideology and self-image. To lead them, it is helpful to know which you are dealing with.

The following is not meant to be comprehensive. The team types often overlap, so we are constantly finding new tribes and subtribes. For example, Will Wright's team at EA and Jonathan Neale and his colleagues at McLaren can be labeled as creative, techie, and problem-solving. Nor is it intended as a typology. Rather, it illustrates the range of tasks that clever teams must deal with and the particular challenges or problems that come with them.

TECHIE TEAMS

Once the preserve of high-tech companies, today techie teams are everywhere. They include computer game designers at Electronic Arts, software programmers at Microsoft, and the inevitable Googlets. But techie teams also occur in financial services companies, such as ING and Deutsche Bank, where technology increasingly resides in the organizational engine room. Indeed, IT and operations have moved from being support services in global banks to being at the heart of the business. For example, Deutsche Bank's expertise at processing foreign exchange has given the bank a real competitive advantage.

Techie teams are prone to four distinct challenges. First, clever techies have a tendency to be overly specialized. They are recognized as experts in their own field, and their clever status often rests on this. They have no wish to be led elsewhere.

Here is the consultant Paul Glen, drawing directly on his own work experience: "In general, geeks are rather ambivalent about joining groups. As introverts, they're most comfortable working alone, concentrating on problems small enough to be attacked by only one person . . . The most common problem is the team that's comprised solely of people who are strong at individual task skills and lack even a basic awareness of the other (relationship, teamwork, process) skills."[5]

Jonathan Neale acutely observes the following about the technically skilled engineers at the core of McLaren's success. He describes the tension between shared mission and freedom to act: "The engineers like to be led by people who are authentic and gifted. The challenges are being able to give the technical team a sense of ownership about the mission. This has to be articulated in a language that describes their degrees of freedom to act and, simultaneously, the constraint or obligation to come back and report on it. So, they all want light-touch management, and they all want more funds and say, just trust us, it will be all right on the night. We don't work like that. They're accountable too."

This leads to a second, related problem: individual team members are typically obsessed by their own particular specialty, which can work to the detriment of the overall team objective. If each team member focuses on their particular part of the jigsaw puzzle, they may never put all the pieces together to see the bigger picture. Two plus two does not necessarily add up.

We have observed many occasions in the pharmaceutical sector where technically excellent teams beaver away on their specialty and lose sight of the overall picture of drug development. At Roche we observed how CEO of the pharmaceuticals division Bill Burns's deep knowledge of the marketplace helped to pull back technical teams from the danger of overspecialization. Similarly, in the IT world, it is commonplace to find IT professionals dedicating large parts of their spare time to IT-related hobbies and passions.

Third, where the technology is a facilitator of other business goals, as with a financial services company, for example, this narrow obsession compounds a tendency for techie teams to have a low level of identification with the mainstream organization. Think back to Will Wright's comments on his relationship with Electronic Arts: "You say Electronic Arts, but to me that doesn't have much meaning." So, while the leader may be under pressure to deliver on commercial goals, the team may fall in love with the technology for its own sake.

"Part of the problem is that though there are very clever people in IT, often they cannot translate that into the business. You have a language problem. But you also have it on the business side—guys that are very clever on the business side, but have no clue on the operations side, on how to do it," observes ING's Neil Buckley. "How do you bridge that gap? That's part of what we struggle with constantly, and until companies realize that technology is something they can't live without, need to embrace, keep control of, understand, and make work for them, it won't change."

The fourth, and somewhat clichéd, problem is that many techies have weak interpersonal skills. One programmer we spoke to admitted that the commonest means of communicating with his colleagues in his open-plan office was instant messaging rather than conversation. This is the stereotypical view of the computer geek, of course, but as with many stereotypes, there is a large grain of truth to it. Here's how self-confessed geek Paul Glen sums it up: "The image of the lonely nerd is now firmly established in our culture. And although it's not true for all geeks, it does carry a kernel of truth . . . given a choice between spending time with technology or with people, they generally choose technology . . . Geeks aren't interested in teasing apart the complexity of another person's strengths or weakness and how to leverage or mitigate them. They just want to judge and move on."[6]

It should be added that this isn't the sole preserve of clever people in this particular sector. "A lot of clever people are not clever in social dynamics. They lack emotional intelligence. They lack a repertoire of social skills to influence things. Because they can't figure out how to influence things this way, they sometimes look for rules to protect them," one leader commented. (More about the clever rule book in part 3.)

Neil Buckley of ING tries to encourage his team toward greater self-reflection: "Before you can do anything in any role, you have to really understand who you are, what you bring to the table— your own strengths and weaknesses. Until you've done that, you don't know how you can blend and mix with other people."

One of our interviewees told us about a senior analyst who was simply not a good people manager. "It kills me to have me say that, but he is a bad manager," she told us. "His idea of solving a problem is, oh, I won't tell the analyst who read it. I'll do an all-nighter and fix it. So you wind up with people thinking that they're doing great, and then they're hearing on the outside that maybe they're not and nobody's giving them that direction. So opening that communication is a big challenge of mine."

This compounds the separation and specialization issues, and can cause clever people to be isolated from their colleagues. Often they speak their own language—"geekspeak" in the IT world which makes it difficult for the team to connect with other parts of the organization. (As we shall see in chapter 4, it is here that the leader can play a vital role by acting as a bridge and interface with other parts of the organization.)

CREATIVE TEAMS

These teams consist of individuals who define themselves in terms of their creativity. Like techie teams, creative teams see themselves as distinct from the commercial culture of the organization. They may be suspicious or even scornful of people they regard as *suits*. Creative teams are to be found in a variety of places, including media organizations, such as the BBC and CNN, and advertising and marketing companies, such as WPP.

Creative teams are prone to four slightly different problems. First, as Belbin observed many years back, the most creative member of the team tends to dominate. Unless they are handled carefully, other team members may become frustrated—and even sulk.

The second challenge with creatives is that they are drawn to novelty at the expense of quality. So they confuse new ideas with good new ideas. These are the people who might suggest mountaineering holidays in the Netherlands or a beach break in Nebraska.

The third characteristic of creative teams is that, in common with techie teams, they often do not see their work in a commercial context. They want to do the best—and hence most creative—work regardless of cost. As a result, they don't always think commercially, regarding themselves as a creative team rather than a creative *business* team. Controlling program-making budgets at any TV station is a constant struggle, with each side reinforcing its stereotypes of the other—suits who see only cost, and creatives who are perceived to live in a world of their own. It's the same in an advertising agency that needs to work to a client's budget but where the creatives want to produce award-winning ads. The two goals may be compatible, but it requires skillful leadership to accomplish them.

Bernard Arnault, the man who gave us a whole new generation of designers—including John Galliano at Dior and Marc Jacobs at Vuitton—is clear about the challenge: "Designers here know that they have the freedom to create, they are not controlled by others.

But then ideas have to be a commercial success. Designers are artists, but artists who have to make sales."[7]

In addition, the creatives at LVMH are reminded that their role is to serve the brand. As Pierre-Yves Roussel of LVMH puts it, "When I am putting together a team, the first thing is fit with the brand. Each brand has its own personality—and it's always more important than the creative people. It's there forever. Some brands are 160 years old. Our job is to nurture and grow them. We must make sure to cast creative talent to fit the brand."

Finally, while creative tension can be a positive (and even necessary) force, passions run high in creative teams. Individual members are likely to come into conflict with each other in ways that move beyond differences in opinion about the task and stray into personal conflict. They can become emotionally highly charged and as a result are prone to blowing up. You can often see this pattern in advertising agencies and design companies, for example. In sociological terms, while cognitive (task) conflict may be productive, too much affective (personal) conflict can render the team dysfunctional.

According to Alain Lorenzo at LVMH, "Some creatives work really well under pressure and some don't. I can think of two of our best-known creatives who were both highly emotional. One was fearful of the real world. He surrounded himself with people who sheltered him. To talk to him, you had to talk to his friends, who would find the right words to talk to him. The other was a loner. He hid his uncertainty behind his aggression. He was the most aggressive person I have ever seen!"

Of course, the creatives often deliberately act out their creative selves. It becomes a kind of elaborate role-playing. Underneath may lurk a more complex reality. We were told this story by the chairman of a major news organization. It concerns the behavior of a globally famous news journalist: an exemplar of the very clever, rather skeptical journalists who drive the news business. He will always imply that he is deeply suspicious of everything the suits are up to and really doesn't understand why they don't just help in the newsroom rather than lounging around in boardrooms. But the reality is rather different—he is astute about the way the company is being led and the strategic direction it is taking. While publicly expressing disdain for the business side of his organization, he privately asks penetrating questions about relationships with important customers and growth prospects. He is also an outspoken champion of the organization when outside it, with politicians, other media colleagues, and customers. You cannot sit him down in a strategy meeting with a sixty-slide PowerPoint presentation, but you would be wise to keep him informed of key developments in the business.

PROFESSIONAL TEAMS

Clever professionals are high-status clevers such as doctors, lawyers, accountants, and academics. They are to be found in a range of organizations, from academic institutions, such as business schools, to corporate law firms, auditors, and hospitals. What they all have in common is that, as individuals, they identify more with their profession than with the organization.

Those who lead professional teams face their own special challenges. First, professional teams have a tendency to be willfully naughty. It may sound strange, but in our experience there is no other way to describe it. People who are highly professional and capable individuals in all other aspects of their lives can often behave like children when they are put into teams.

A colleague of ours once astutely observed that when groups of our highly intelligent professorial colleagues were forced to sit together for meetings, it would be a matter of minutes before infantile behavior emerged. This took a variety of forms: surreptitious passing of humorous notes, reading of newspapers, giggling at the back of the room, falling asleep, and so on.

A managing partner of a high-profile law firm regularly complained to us of how his senior partner colleagues "acted like children" in their monthly executive meetings. They, in turn, remarked privately, that the managing partner behaved like a headmaster. And so the loop was unproductively reinforced.

A senior medical professional told us of what happened right at the start of his new job. There had been a problem in a particular specialty, so he held a meeting with everyone involved, and a proposed solution was agreed on. Two days later, he received a letter from the three senior consultants in the specialty. They said that they'd given it further thought and had changed their minds. "I just thought, my first week in the job, and I'm going to have to go back to the board and say, I had a solution and I haven't fixed it," the leader told us. "And I started thinking, how on earth do I handle this. You can't tell consultants what to do. In the end, I wrote a letter saying, thank you for your letter, I've noted what you say. I think your behavior is completely unprofessional. We had a meeting, we agreed [on] this course of action, and I see no reason to change the course of action; now, please, will you get on and implement it. Basically, nothing happened. They just got on and did it. I learnt a really, really big lesson that day."

The conceptual distinction is this: professionals exhibit high degrees of self-discipline—without it, they cannot qualify or practice—yet they often display staggeringly low levels of social discipline.

This is compounded by (or perhaps is simply a defense mechanism for) a second characteristic: doctors, lawyers, accountants (even business school professors!) seek to avoid feedback. In part this comes from their high status, which makes them highly sensitive to losing face in front of their peers. But in more basic terms, the professions "profess" to know best. They do in a literal sense see themselves as "clever." All the more painful, then, to receive evidence that they may not be quite as clever as they thought.

Their third characteristic is an obsession with client or specialist peer relationships. This means that clever professionals often regard themselves as being in competition with their clever colleagues within the organization, but often in other specialties. This can be a major obstacle to collaboration. In the big accounting firms, partners will often feel as if they own the relationship with a client—making them reluctant to cross-sell services from other parts of the firm.

Nowhere, perhaps, is this obsession with specialty more prominently displayed than in the relationships among health service professionals—or with such costly outcomes in terms of money and lives. Here are the conclusions of a U.S. research study: "Coordination and communication among specialties, functions, and roles in hospitals plays a very large and generally unrecognized role in health care quality outcomes. Furthermore, due to the barriers of organizational boundaries, status and expertise that divide health care providers from each other, the relationships that facilitate the coordination of interdependent work are particularly hard to achieve."[8]

Why are such relationships hard to achieve if they deliver better health care? The research goes on to observe, "At their best, experts stand for high standards of service and scientifically proven knowledge . . . at their worst, their obsessive qualities make experts into inflexible know-it-alls. Physician experts want health centers and hospitals to serve them and they do not appreciate the added value of an organization over what they do as individuals. Physicians, like other experts, relate best with mentors, peers, or younger high-potential apprentices who share their values."

In health care, malfunctioning teams can make the difference between life and death. Elsewhere in professional teams, the implications may be less severe, but the behavior is frequently much the same.

And there is more. The fourth characteristic of professional teams is a tendency to be overly concerned or pedantic about setting rules and norms—something that comes from professional training. Splitting hairs is their modus operandi. This can take up huge amounts of time and energy, which obviously detracts from effective performance. Indeed, there is an irony here. Whereas clever people—professionals included—will regularly claim that they wish for relatively few rules, which are agreed on rather than imposed, they often tie themselves up with procedural rules that control entry and standards. Witness the gargantuan bureaucracy that surrounds the appointments committees of universities or the admissions procedures to partnership at the major accounting firms.

PROBLEM-SOLVING TEAMS

Ask EA's Will Wright what sort of team he is leading, and he is likely to categorize it under problem solving. Indeed, the problem-solving element is a key attractor for star programmers. After all, programmers could probably earn more money working for a bank than they do working on something like his *Spore* project. "To be able to work on interesting problems is probably the single most interesting thing for people here. I think what they really enjoy is solving a problem that, from their point of view, nobody else has solved before. Exploring a solution set that has not been well explored feels very significant to them. I think it also gives them a lot of ownership over their work. In fact, we are inventing our own problems and trying to make the problem solving entertaining from the consumer's point of view," Wright told us.

Problem-solving teams overlap with several of the other clever teams. For example, creative teams or techie teams are often also problem-solving teams. But there is also a distinct type of organization that relies on problem-solving teams. I think of an architectural practice such as Arup, an engineering company such as ABB, or an IT services provider such as Fujitsu. In each of these organizations, teams of clevers are given big problems to solve, and create huge amounts of value by doing so.

As with other clever teams, problem-solving teams can create huge amounts of value, but they also come with their own baggage. In particular, we have observed three distinct tendencies.

First, they only like big problems—which require correspondingly grand solutions. It is this obsession with the grand that demarcates them as a type of clever team.

When Arup was commissioned to design a new bridge across the Thames in London to commemorate the millennium, for example, the clever team of architects came up with a pioneering new design. The £18.2 million Millennium Bridge, central London's first new river crossing in more than a century, opened on June 10, 2000. However, it began swaying alarmingly when there was a very high volume of people crossing it at the same time—a problem the engineers attributed to "synchronized footfall."

The problem was not life threatening, but the bridge was quickly dubbed the "Wobbly Bridge" by the media, and was closed to the public amid a blaze of negative publicity. If ever there was a problem that required solving, this was it. A team of architects and engineers at Arup was given the brief to tackle it. They quickly recognized that there were two possible approaches. The cheapest (and least elegant) fix was to bolt on a stabilizing structure to the existing structure. The second, and much more expensive, solution involved the installation of ninety-one individual dampers, similar to car shock absorbers, designed to reduce the movement of the 350-meter bridge.

Which solution did they opt for? Option two, of course, because it was a bigger challenge. In February 2002, the Millennium Bridge Trust announced that it had raised the £5 million required to carry out the recommended modifications. The story has an even more positive ending. As the global director of research, Jeremy Watson, told us, "Not only did we solve the problem, but we developed a new product range from the solution!"

The second thing about problem-solving teams is, they are perfectionists. As such, they are inclined to pursue the most elegant solution regardless of cost. When BAA was privatized to run the United Kingdom's airports, senior executives had a tough time convincing the airport runway team to stop pursuing its objective of perfect runways. The commercial reality is that the difference in cost between perfection and thoroughly adequate is huge.

The third problem is that problem-solving teams are often problem junkies and are constantly looking for new problems to solve. For their leader, this can be both infuriating and commercially challenging.

STRATEGY TEAMS

Strategy teams are a specialized type of problem-solving team. To many in the business world, strategy formulation is the pinnacle of intellectual endeavor. In the 1960s and 1970s, regiments of bright young graduates were paid to sit in corporate strategic-planning departments and create five-year plans. Today, the dedicated corporate strategists are fewer in number—but, arguably, cleverer than ever.

Some are busy identifying potential targets for M&A activity, while others are scoping out new markets in emerging economies, or plotting the likely outcome of industry deregulation or the effects of political change. The top strategy consulting firms, such as McKinsey & Company, The Boston Consulting Group, and Bain & Company, also employ some of the smartest MBA graduates in the world.

One of the most impressive people we met was Jim Singh. Born in British Guyana, Singh studied in Canada and trained as a management accountant. He worked at Booker McConnell and then in a rubber company before joining Nestlé in 1977. He worked in Nestlé Canada, where he became CFO. "When I joined, it was less than a C$200 million company and when I left it was C$2 billion. I actually grew up with the company," he says. He then moved to Nestlé headquarters in Switzerland, where he became head of acquisitions and business development.

Jim Singh's team is relatively small, around a dozen people. Singh's approach is built on openness, flexibility, and sensitivity to the team's makeup. "We could not do our work unless we were really the model for teamwork. I beg, borrow, and steal; I can't command, really don't have direct authority. We have to be a model of how to work as a team," he says. "You have to give the team the leverage and the room to tell you things that you don't want to hear, or you didn't expect to hear. You need to be as much a member of the team as a leader, not forgetting that somebody has to lead and take ultimate responsibility. Once you're a member of the team, you have to share because you're either receiving or giving information. There's got to be some sharing and there's got to be some openness to say whether you feel that you're adding value, you're not, or people are not giving you what you want. You need to create that sense of openness where people set aside their ego, which is difficult to do, but listen to what other people are saying."

The problems with strategy teams are fourfold. First, strategists have a tendency to be elitist, regarding themselves as the intellectual superiors of their operational colleagues. This can lead to hubris—made worse by an obstinate refusal to admit mistakes.

"Some people come and say, that guy's great but he's high maintenance," says Nestlé's Singh. "And I say, well, did you talk to him? I don't think I should, because he's senior to me. I say, no, when you're a member of a team, everybody's equal. There's going to be a leader, but everybody's a member of the team. You can't have a weak link, so don't come to me and lay everything down on me; you have to go and lay it on your colleague and make sure you understand each other."

Second, they can easily become disconnected from the sharp end of the business, creating strategy in a vacuum that cannot be implemented. In recent years, this has led to a backlash, with more attention paid to execution; witness, for example, the number of business books with *execution* in the title.

The third problem with strategy teams is that they are heavily reliant on data. Unlike creative teams, which are high on emotional energy and passion, strategy teams are predominantly rational in their approach. Too little information, and they are unable to draw any conclusions; and too much, and they can suffer from a paralysis of analysis.

This is compounded by the fourth problem: their thoroughness can make them seem ponderous and unwilling to draw quick conclusions. This problem is exacerbated by the speed with which the global economy now moves, which can render data—and their strategic analysis—irrelevant overnight.

Good examples of strategic clever teams include those found at some of the large consulting firms. At one well known firm the emphasis is on inculcating a set of values that become the context in which a person works, the context in which the person thinks, and the context in which they allow themselves to be directed.

"This is a very values-driven organization. The kind of people that we hire typically are more values driven, they're more driven by ideals and aspirations," reflects one senior partner. "In our recruiting process the question we really ask is, Do you want to work with this person? And unless every recruiter says yes, you don't hire the guy. He might be very, very smart, but if the recruiter doesn't really want to work with the guy, he doesn't get hired."

In practice, team working in this firm's culture combines flexibility with rigorous standards—and enforcement. "At any point you're probably touching directly a total of between ten and twenty people—we don't have people who report to you. For the time that they work with you, you provide them an evaluation, but every six months everyone they work with provides them with an evaluation, and that's in addition to evaluation by peers, evaluation by people who report to you or who work with you. That then goes to an evaluation committee of a group of partners in the office. You take input from each of the people you work with; no one person has a great say in the evaluation of that particular individual. You develop by giving people feedback."

This firm regards itself as a caring meritocracy. In practice, this is more a forthright statement of intent than touchy-feely and humanitarian. "By constantly exposing to people what they could do better—be it around problem solving or communication—you're propelling them forward, and a lot of people just don't like to see that they can do things better." The logic is that if people are stagnating in terms of their development, they take resources and attention away from the people who are developing. It doesn't want people taking opportunities who are not making the best use of them.

We asked a partner what motivates the clever people he works with. He pinpoints two factors:

> One is recognition. Recognition not to say you're a clever guy, but recognition that what they're doing is having impact. I have seen consultants in projects where they leave by six o'clock every day, they probably go and watch movies or exercise, their weekends are completely free, their work plan is very straightforward, and they're just completely bored and fed up. And I've seen teams of people working until three o'clock in the morning, every day, not sleeping, working through all their weekends, exhausted, no clear direction on where they're really going, but they're loving every moment of it. And I think it's a feeling of achievement.
>
> The second thing is change. I've seen that after six months of doing the same thing, a typical consultant is just fed up with it and just wants to do something else, wants a new challenge, wants the next problem, because it's the process of discovering a solution to a problem that they find interesting, and solving the same problem two or three or four times is no longer interesting because they know how to do it. The mechanics are less fun than figuring out the mechanics.

TOP TEAMS

Among the most visible and yet, curiously, least understood clever teams are senior management teams. Think of the average corporate board, for example. It consists of a group of very clever strong-willed people who meet infrequently, and includes a number of outsiders, sometimes with little practical experience of the industry or the company. They are thrown together half a dozen times a year, with vague performance objectives, and are expected to provide decisive leadership and deliver corporate performance to exacting governance standards. Then we wonder why it sometimes goes wrong.

The board is simply the most extreme example of a top team. The reality is that, despite a lot of research and wise words from experienced senior managers, how top teams can and should work effectively is relatively underresearched. While team members are charged with responsibility for delivering both financial performance and effective governance, the human dynamics at work in top teams are sometimes barely acknowledged.

Getting the best from top teams, we believe, starts with a better understanding of their sociological dimensions. Over the past decade, we have worked with more than twenty boards of major corporations and have interviewed many more CEOs in an effort to better understand how they behave. Our conclusion is that top teams are complex social systems. They suffer from four specific problems.

First, the balance between relationships and performance (what we have referred to in earlier work as sociability and solidarity) is often unstable. Too much emphasis on relationships, for instance, can lead to a lack of accountability. No one wants to fire their friend. But if the pendulum moves too far the other way, too much emphasis on short-term financial results at the expense of team cohesion can result in an overly aggressive (and defensive) culture. Fearful of personal blame, individual team members end up worrying about their own performance targets instead of the wider organizational objectives. It's a short step from here to the turf protection and silo-related divisiveness that we referred to in our discussion of interdependence and shared objectives.

The second issue is that the people promoted to top teams get there because they are good at looking for and living with complexity. But once they reach the top, they need to simplify. Many top teams do not make this adjustment and become out of touch with the rest of the organization. When Niall FitzGerald was chairman of Unilever, he often observed that he had fifty clever people bombarding him with data every day—genetically modified crops, the euro zone, strategies for developing in emerging economies—and yet his task was to keep focused on where Unilever needed to be five or seven years into the future. Once teams are at the top, the task becomes one of simplification.

A third problem is the failure of top teams to properly utilize the clever resources that are available to them. We have seen this issue in a particularly pronounced way with the deployment of independent directors on boards. Often recruited with considerable rigor—and expensive headhunters—independent directors arrive with typically impeccable credentials. Yet their experience and expertise is regularly underutilized. Over recent years, we have surveyed the functioning of boards of major organizations, both public and private. Of the many dimensions we have measured, the area of least satisfaction, as expressed by board members themselves, is the exploitation of the expertise of independents. Only very skillful chairmen seem able to overcome this recurring problem—through careful control of the agenda, sensitive orchestration of board meetings, and building of connections between independents and executives outside board meetings.

UNIQUELY SIMILAR

Now that we have identified some of the different types of clever teams that we have observed, what does this mean for the people who have to lead them? We began by stressing that teams are characterized by shared goals, interdependence, and awareness of each other. For all of the types of clever teams we have described, these remain the essential challenges. Leaders must inculcate shared goals, build interdependence, and increase awareness among a population not obviously predisposed to any of these. In the next chapter, we discuss the fundamental issues involved in decoding clever teams so that they might reach their full potential.

BREAKING THE CODE
OF CLEVER TEAMS

N CHAPTER 3, WE LISTED lots of issues that seem to arise when you bring clever people together to work in teams, and, as we showed, there are a variety of clever teams that exhibit different kinds of problems. These issues revolve around the tension between answering, "What needs to be done?" and the critically important "How should we do it?"

Now, we'd like to be more positive and suggest some leadership actions, which can help clever teams to perform more effectively. In order to do this, we must be absolutely clear that we have adequately diagnosed the underlying problem. At its core, the issue is this: there is a fundamental contradiction between the social processes characteristic of clever teams and the necessary characteristics of their work. Let's try to explain this.

Clever teams are normally engaged in tasks with the following characteristics. First, they are complex. There would be little point in bringing clever people together into teams in order to tackle simple tasks or tasks that could be routinized. The complexity involves many interfaces, high levels of uncertainty, and value chains, which may extend not only beyond the team but beyond the organization.

Second, clever teams are often deployed in dynamic environments—that is to say, many of the variables that they are dealing with are moving around rapidly and unpredictably. As a result, this complexity and rapid change typically requires highly cohesive teams able to exploit different forms of cleverness and to work together over long periods of time. Without cohesiveness, the presence of complexity and change could produce chaos and fragmentation.

So far, so good. Surely, having cohesive teams is a laudable outcome. But the nature of the tasks that clever teams are engaged in requires almost the opposite of cohesion—even a degree of fragmentation. Here are some of the characteristics of their work:

- **It requires diversity.** Creativity increases with diversity and declines with homogeneity. This is not just diversity measured in conventional HR ways (though, of course, that's important enough) but diversity of perspective. Only this can generate the high levels of cognitive conflict that clever teams require. On many occasions, we have witnessed the diversity of top teams in the City of London. They are made up of self-made entrepreneurial salesmen ("barrow boys" in the English vernacular) and supremely well-educated Oxbridge graduates—but they often demonstrate high levels of creativity.

- **It is characterized by serendipity.** Because the many variables clever teams deal with have rapidly changing coefficients, there is always the possibility of unintended consequences and surprises. Glaxo had a strategy to become the world's leading cardiovascular drug company and then discovered Zantac (the antiulcer drug). Indeed, it was this drug that transformed Glaxo into arguably the world's greatest pharmaceutical company. The CD, which in the 1980s was the savior of the recorded music industry, was developed as a computer storage device. Clever industries are full of such examples.

- **It inevitably involves multiple interfaces.** The very nature of the complex problems clever teams deal with requires that they handle many relationships outside of their immediate team. No drug can be developed without managing such interfaces.

Given the characteristics above, clever teams are volatile. The requirement for the clash of ideas, the passion that they bring to their work, and high levels of intrinsic uncertainty are all conditions that generate volatility. Remember, for example, the volatile reactions of designers at LVMH to differing degrees of pressure. At Island Records, executives would come close to a fistfight over which single to take off an album. They really cared.

GLUE TROUBLE

All of these characteristics sit uneasily with some aspects of high levels of team cohesion. Aggressive opportunists from a broad range of backgrounds don't sound like a dream team. Indeed, the leader may need to deconstruct the concept of cohesiveness. Some aspects are helpful. The shared emotion generates high levels of energy. Cohesive teams tend to have shared values—again, helpful to performance. Cohesion increases the chances of widespread collaboration among team members.

But there are aspects of cohesiveness that the leader must mitigate. The most dangerous is the tendency of cohesive teams to exclusivity—a kind of collective introspection. This is dangerous because clever teams facing complex tasks need to be outward looking, constantly exploring the edges of the difficult problems they are trying to solve. One of the most striking observations from our conversations with clever teams was the number of times that clever teams were remarkably lacking in curiosity about the world around them and the wider aspects of the problems they were trying to solve. If there was one common lament that we heard, it was this: from team members, that their leaders failed to understand the complexity of their work; and from team leaders, that their team failed to see the bigger picture.

There are other negative symptoms of the excessive cohesiveness. There is a horrible danger of the team's coming to believe its own propaganda, generating the view that the team is invulnerable—that no problem is beyond them. Connected to this is a dismissive attitude to the competition.

The team leader must resist these negative symptoms by relentlessly feeding in data and insight from outside the team and indeed from outside the organization. The leader must introduce continuous levels of cognitive conflict, sometimes by changing team members. All of this will reduce the negative aspects of cohesiveness.

THE SAME GAME

Conventional wisdom suggests that if you want creative solutions, then you need to build diversity into teams. Research suggests that creativity increases with diversity and declines with sameness. But diversity itself raises problems. If there is too much diversity, the team falls apart. There is not enough in common to make them cohere. If there is too little, we get contented teams that lack creativity and the high levels of cognitive conflict that are the lifeblood of clever teams. For the leader, this translates into the challenge of balancing a necessary degree of cohesion with the stimulation of cognitive conflict. In addition, the leader needs to provide both direction and discipline. We must never fall into the trap of believing that clever teams should be indulged.

The underlying processes that produce these effects are as follows. People who are similar usually find it easier to work with one another, have relationships that the leader can read, and form teams that bond quickly and produce results. As a result, it is tempting for a leader to build homogeneous teams. Lookalikes are always a convenient and comfortable recruitment option. But it has been shown that highly diverse groups, though they often underperform homogeneous teams initially, can outperform in the longer term, once they have learned to cohere and take advantage of their wider range of experience and ideas. For the tasks relevant to clever teams, diversity is the route to follow.

The traditional approach to diversity is to look at it from the perspective of gender, religion, culture, and so on. This is worthy but not sufficient. In reality what clever teams (and all teams) thrive on is not diversity of background but diversity of perspective. Conventional measures of diversity only go so far. The comfort zone is to err on the side of homogeneity.

PICKING YOUR OWN

In our experience, the best clever teams are not designed; they find each other. Clevers are typically very good at spotting other clevers they want to work with, so one approach is to let them self-select as much as possible. We have seen this work in design consultancies, academic institutions, and luxury goods businesses. This will require a huge leap of faith for a traditional HR department but can generate energy and real high performance. But this strategy also carries with it important responsibilities. The leader cannot abdicate responsibility for performance. Self-selection without discipline is likely to end in failure. This, we believe, goes some way to explaining the tendency of successful clevers to fail when they are overindulged.

Self-selection is our preferred approach. But sometimes creating diversity of perspective requires intervention. Where teams are engineered for diversity, they must be carefully handled. One of the most interesting leaders of a clever team we encountered was Marc

Silvester, chief technology officer of Fujitsu Services. Silvester's direct team numbers just over one hundred people. Half have years of technical and service experience. They have been selected for their maverick tendencies, their willingness to challenge and change, to voice their views. The other half of the team, recruited over eighteen months, has been specifically recruited from outside the technology sector. The logic is simple. "You don't get exceptional change and innovation from like-minded static-thinking people, and that's why we have a group like mine, which is where you put together odd people, people that have got their own passion, people that are really special for something; they just haven't worked out what that something is," says Silvester.

In the previous year, plastic surgeons, venture capitalists, a member of a professional helicopter display team, a national radio presenter, a Westminster lobbyist, and two former soldiers from the United Kingdom's crack Special Air Service (SAS) regiment were among those recruited to the team. "They are people at the top of their field, but nothing at all to do with this industry," says Silvester. "There are a hell of a lot of challenges in managing my team, and a lot of guidance and a lot of support, and a huge amount of personal emotion that goes into bringing people on to be the person that they can be. We all trade our weaknesses and our strengths, every single one of us across the whole team."

How do you recruit such an eclectic bunch of clevers? It isn't easy. Marc Silvester explains:

> They were recruited through Mensa [an organization for people whose IQs are in the top two percent of the population]. I employed a specialist company to go and find people at the top of their career blocked by their vision. We spent two years doing it. I got a seventy percent hit rate. Three have had to go because they are the wacky scientists that could never really make the step into the next application of their thoughts. But if you compare that model with traditional recruitment, it usually has around about a thirty

percent hit rate. So we built a program with an outside company that looks specifically at identifying those types of people, and they can come from any walk of life except the IT industry. They are not allowed into the first interview if they've got any inherent knowledge, experience, or job relating to IT. I don't want them because I can teach them IT. I can't teach them how to be innovative or how to be inspirational in their own life. They'll have that, it's natural, or they won't.

THE DISCIPLINE OF TEAMS

Of course, it is one thing to design a team on paper or even to allow clevers to self-select their team, and quite another to get it to gel together in the real world—ask any sports coach or anyone who has picked a fantasy soccer team. Teams take work, design, and a leader's time. They are, after all, an important and valuable investment. The common assumption is that labeling a collection of individuals a "team" leads automatically to the group working as a team. The reality is usually more difficult. In part, this is because relationships have to be built between each member of the team. That takes both time and careful handling.

Says Marc Silvester:

> From my experience of watching other teams, I will have people that other parts of the organization can't understand, don't appreciate, probably think are a problem. There is talent absolutely everywhere. They just haven't been given the chance to find the best way of bringing that to a different activity. Around ten people are in the team because other people have got challenges. Probably thirty or forty have been found. Probably another twenty are individuals that just need to be inspired and led and given the opportunity to do what they always knew they could do. So they come into the team as well.

Those are the ones you have to watch because they are passion led, not process led, and at some point passion is a killer, and process has to move into play because they will find any route through any organization just based on the fact that they are interested in what they want to get done, but it will never get done. You have to recognize that in people and move it out of their hands and into other people's hands who just excel at getting it completed.

What Silvester is alluding to is the need to take projects away from clever teams at certain points. This is a topic that recurred again and again in our conversations with successful leaders of clever teams. This sort of discipline can seem harsh, but sometimes it is about being cruel to be kind—not just to the organization but to the clevers as individuals. Silvester explains:

> We have taken things away from some people because it's a self-destruct. For some of these big projects, it can be a real sort of career-ending activity for them. But helping them recognize first of all that their value to that idea was where they got it to, they cannot actually deliver it.
>
> That is why we have a lot of rotation inside of my team, so everybody does everything at the drop of a hat and there is no static nature to what we do. All of that is designed to take them to the edge of the cliff, hold them there so that they can enjoy the experience of looking down. It's not necessarily a threat, but also they come back from that looking at life slightly differently, and they know where the boundaries are and can enjoy the boundary and then know exactly how far they can push themselves the next step forward.

Discipline is perhaps the most underrated leadership skill of all. Our failure to recognize this in part arises from the dominant Western conception of freedom. In this tradition, freedom is conceptualized as the absence of constraint. The fewer the constraints, the more free you are. There is another view of freedom, which regards a degree of constraint as a condition of human freedom. The question then becomes, "Which degree of constraint maximizes the freedom of the clever team?" This tradition finds its expression in works as different as Thomas Hobbes's *Leviathan*, with its insistence on the state as a guardian of individual freedom, and in Baruch Spinoza's tantalizingly cryptic remark that freedom is "knowledge of necessity."

Whether you are the president of the United States or the leader of a local youth club, you operate within constraints. Great leaders accept this as the challenge. Only bad leaders blame the limitations of the situation. For leaders of clever teams, constraints typically do not have to do with resources (most clever teams are well funded). Rather, they have to do with commercial or organizational requirements. In short, leaders have to bring a product to market or deliver to a deadline.

As Tristram Carfrae, an Arup board member and world-renowned engineer, perceptively remarks, "One of the things I am proud of is instilling in the creative building engineers the idea that by teaming up with a project manager, it makes their lives *better*—it gives them *more* freedom."

But discipline is not just about the endgame. It is intrinsic to every decision the clever team makes—and its culture. As Will Wright explains:

Every design decision that we make is going to reflect whether we think we are doing a spreadsheet or something that's entertainment. How the animators choose to animate something, the way the sound designers put a voice to something or sound effects, the colors that we choose—every little thing that we do reflects the mood of the team, what they are thinking of as they design it. It is something that we have to remind ourselves of continually; every now and then we will get bogged down with something. A lot of times we will hit these fairly intractable design problems. 'How can we make this work with that?' We're going to have to do something that totally breaks reality or doesn't make sense, and then we'll attack it with humor in the game design.

There is a discipline that comes from consistency of approach and even philosophy. One of the jewels in the crown of the BBC, perhaps the world's most creative broadcaster, is its Natural History Unit, producer of epic programs like *Blue Planet* and *Life on Earth*. It is located in Bristol, a long way from the head office in London, and because of its almost unbroken record of success, it is largely left alone by the corporate apparatchiks. This is just as well, because the members of the unit are rather uninterested in both the grand vision of the BBC and its wider corporate purpose. They are interested in, maybe obsessed with, world-class nature programs. They have aims (indeed, there is a map of the world with many pins in it where they plan their future programs) and direction. Their passion for excellence makes them intolerant of anything less than the best. They are perhaps the best example we have seen of a self-directing clever team. Pulling in the opposite direction is serendipity—random good fortune.

DESIGN FOR SERENDIPITY

Leaders have long understood that they have to provide vision and clear goals. Indeed, it has become a cliché. But in the case of clever teams, setting direction involves a more subtle role. Bland visions have little meaning for clevers, yet they need clear direction.

Microsoft's European development center is located in a stunning science park just outside Dublin, Ireland. The place is full of very clever people. If you ever want to sample the global nature of a giant knowledge-based business, then visit them. While there, we met a young Spanish mathematician, a Polish professor, an American exemplar of all that's most exciting about Silicon Valley, and many more. They are hugely energetic and lucid about how you structure for creativity and innovation. But not one mentioned the wider vision of Microsoft. It had much more to do with the next big difficult problem and with the deadlines and deliverables that went along with this. This is not to suggest for a moment a cohort of clever automatons; rather, they embraced their difficult problems with agility and opportunism. Leaders of clever teams must set a clear direction but also remain open to unexpected opportunities. Serendipity is a vital element of clever work and should not be squashed.

Remember, Will Wright's inspiration for *SimCity* came from his work on an entirely different game project that involved his playing with a mapmaking tool. Had the leader of the project insisted that he leave what he was doing and get on with the project at hand, perhaps the *Sims* phenomenon would never have happened. Today, Wright faces the same sort of challenge in producing *Spore*. No one is better qualified to understand the subtle nuances of direction setting for clever teams.

So, how does a studio led by a brilliant games designer work? It begins, says Wright, with a sense of shared objectives. At the very beginning of a project, he gets the core team to buy into the same model of what they want to build. At this stage, he wants people on the same basic page. Of course, pages can change or be ripped up as the project develops.

Lucy Bradshaw, a *Sims* veteran, is executive producer of *Spore* and the person Wright looks to for operational expertise. "Something that Electronic Arts has really spent a lot of time on is figuring out [how] to help creative teams have some structure to understand where they are, to reflect upon what it is that they are making, and to be clear once you get to the production phase," she explains. "After all, it is a business; we are about ultimately producing a commercial product, so you really do need some amount of predictability. The early phase is so formative and can dramatically affect the production phase, where you have a much larger team involved, so you want to make sure you are trying everything that you can and giving tools to that really creative early team to understand what direction we're heading."

To steer progress, Wright helped create a "*Spore* canon" with a vision for each of the games in *Spore*. These were then printed out on large poster-size paper and decorate the studio walls. They are a route map through the game's twists and turns. Some include graphs showing where a player should be after one or two hours of play. This constant aide-mémoire focuses the team working on that particular game and helps other team members figure out how each part relates to the other.

Wright's *Spore* team has a flexible element. Meetings are minimized. People can work at home. (Interestingly, it is the most talented who take particular advantage of this.) There is what Wright calls "a cellular structure." Tasks are broken down so that teams of four to six can work on them. There might be an artist, a couple of programmers, a producer, and a designer in a cell. "You have people with totally different workflows, totally different languages. It is up to those small cell groups to decide if they are going to have weekly meetings or a daily get-together. You want that lower-level, self-organizing thing rather than saying from the top, everybody should talk to their coworkers twice a day." The collective team meets once a week, when anyone can demo what they have been working on.

Where does flexibility meet the formulaic? We asked Lucy Bradshaw about her views on team building. She replies:

First, I think it is about understanding what phase you are in and building a team that has a high degree of skill, passion, and capabilities. Then it is really attributing a sense of ownership so they are driving that process forward; helping them see the progress that they are making; driving communication and reflection about what we have just done; thinking how do we learn from that so, moving forward, we are actually building from the body of work we have just done.

Eventually, it is about bringing on and enlarging the team. Once you get to the point where you are growing, it is about helping create a structure that fosters communication and ownership yet ties it back. There is structure that needs to be developed; there is recognition that you are entering a new phase, communication to those leaders that we are now going into the next phase; we are going to be operating differently. I think if people don't have expectations of what that is going to be like, it can be very jarring going from one phase of the project to the next.

Inevitably, not all groups are created equal—even among a population of the best minds in the company. There are loose cannons—perhaps two groups, says Wright, going through them in his head—likely to stray spectacularly or worryingly. He adds:

Usually 20 percent of what they do I end up having to edit or scratch—it's really cool but it doesn't work. Whereas the other or 30 percent of what they do is stuff that I would never guess they could achieve and has a tremendous upside, disproportionate to the amount of time they spent on it. So they are well worth it. It's typically because that group is really excited about what they're doing, and that is why they end up doing 50 to 60 percent more work than is expected of them, maybe 20 percent of it the wrong direction and 30 percent in a better direction. You want to edit those people very carefully so you don't lose the upside, and you want to be very careful to acknowledge the upside in a broad way so everyone else can see."

THE WISDOM OF LUCK

Clever teams rely on opportunism and serendipity. There are many examples in science and art where new discoveries were the result not of careful planning but of serendipity. Anesthesia, cellophane, cornflakes, dynamite, nylon, PVC, rayon, smallpox vaccine, stainless steel, and Teflon are just some of the innovations that involved fortuitous accidents. Remember too that Arup's resolution of the Millennium Bridge problem produced a new business stream for the company! Yet the role that unplanned incidents play in discovery and invention is often downplayed in business.

Part of the problem is that accidents, by definition, are anathema to business planning, and are therefore not embedded or captured in formal innovation processes and models. As a result, firms do not acknowledge or encourage the sort of serendipitous events that can lead to important breakthroughs. In this regard, clever teams can learn from artists, who often view random events as a vital part of the creative process. Most importantly, perhaps, many artists deliberately inject randomness into their work in the belief that they can acquire the skill for generating useful accidents. It's not irrelevant that artists often expose themselves to new experiences and situations in order to stimulate their creativity. This is as true for Jack Kerouac's *On the Road* as it is for Gauguin's visits to Polynesia.

Serendipity also requires fortuitous collisions. Cross-pollination of ideas is an important aspect of clever teams. Yet, as we noted in the previous chapter, one of the problems with clever teams is their tendency to isolate themselves from their colleagues. In part, this is a result of their ideology, which makes them less interested in the work of their colleagues. This is an area where the leader can make a big difference.

CROSS-STITCH

Clever teams are inclined to be close knit and automatically exclude others. So as the leader, you have to put the stitches in with other parts of the organization.

Let's start with perhaps the easiest and most obvious example, the relationship between R&D and the rest of the organization.

Philips Electronics was one of the most creative researchers in the electronics industry, and yet its relationship with the wider organization limited its ability to bring compelling products to market. Instead, products like Video 2000 (V2000), digital audio tape (DAT), and digital compact cassette (DCC) were technically clever but unrelated to market needs. One of the first actions of the inspirational CEO Jan Timmer was to bring research, development, and marketing people together to share ideas. One of them remarked to us that this was the first time in twenty-five years that he'd been in the same room as a marketer.

In the pharmaceutical sector, the difficult choices are around which compounds go into full development. This process is enormously enhanced by effective communication between the leaders of the research activity and those in development who may need to take the projects on. But it is much more than just the interface between R&D that makes for a great pharmaceutical company. There are interfaces with regulatory affairs, with manufacturing, and, not least, with packaging. Many drugs have failed to reach their full market potential because the interface with packaging wasn't established in a timely manner in the final stages of the development process.

CONNECTED TO THE GRID

McLaren's Formula One team gives us fascinating insights into interface management. As the team prepares for a new season, and a new car, there are at least three distinct phases, all of which require high degrees of cleverness but must be led in a way that connects them.

First, there are the blue-sky dreamers, thinking the unthinkable for the new car. In their relentless pursuit of breakthrough design that will establish clear advantage for the car, they are encouraged to discard last year's orthodoxy. Yet when they have done their work, their design concepts must be passed on to equally clever detail-obsessed producers of blueprints, who will ensure that the dream can be delivered—that the car can be built on time, for the first race of the season. Finally, the car is delivered to race engineers who will ensure that at each and every race the car delivers its maximum performance.

Each of these activities involves technical expertise, insight, and instinct of the highest levels. But if the interfaces between each phase are not effectively led, then disaster beckons. It is the task of leadership in each of the phases to keep information flows at a high level and not to simply throw one part of the process over the wall in the hope that someone will catch it.

It's not just in the technical area where these interfaces are critical. Consider this example. In the music business, the creative process usually begins in the artists and repertoire (A&R) department. Here, decisions to sign artists are made, discussions about musical genres and recording schedules take place, and even the structure of an individual album is resolved. Next comes marketing, where questions about the positioning of the artist are raised, decisions about image and presentation are resolved, and, finally, ad campaigns are initiated. Last comes the sales campaign, when the record hits the streets. Historically, these activities have been horribly unrelated, with each taking place almost in isolation from the adjacent activities. When a record failed, the old cliché was, "It was a great record when it left me." In well-led record companies, marketing and A&R engage in frequent and early conversations so that questions of market positioning can be taken into account when discussing A&R issues. As one record executive told us, "We talk early and often, but we never second-guess an A&R decision."

CUBISM

At legendary consulting engineering company Arup, famous for taking on problems that no one else would touch, interdependence and interface leadership are part of the DNA of the organization. Consider Arup Associates, made up of 120 people based in London.

Architects, engineers, quantity surveyors, and project managers sit in the same room together. If a client comes to them, as if to an architect, they tell them that they will only deploy themselves as a fully integrated team. This spirit even informs giant projects like the creation of the Beijing "Water Cube": the National Aquatics Center built for the Beijing Olympic Games and inspired by the natural formation of soap bubbles.

Tristram Carfrae told us:

> It's attracted attention because it's a fantastic piece of architecture. Because it's a very simple idea that everybody can get hold of. It's a thing that's full of water that looks as though it's made out of bubbles—and actually is! Dead simple. But you can dig into it and find out more. It's not an architectural whimsy. We tried from the engineering side to make it as thermally efficient as can be. Passive solar design for sustainability is to do with getting the sun's energy to heat the pool in the most efficient fashion. That's what caused it to be made out of a transparent material, and it's ETFE (ethylene tetrafluoroethylene) rather than glass because that's better acoustically. We followed an incredible chain almost because we had a collaborative architect. We didn't have a prima donna. So we created a fantastic piece of architecture out of an almost perfect piece of collaboration. You will find every discipline leader on that project is equally proud of their part. There's nobody who is diminished. In this case we made architecture out of functional requirements. Often various bits on the technical or functional side are slaughtered in the name of architecture.

Free of prima donnas, teams can achieve almost anything. Otherwise, they are likely to find themselves blowing bubbles.

We have examined in this second part of the book varieties of clever teams and their pathologies, and suggested some leadership actions that may help. In this chapter, we have explored the tensions between diversity and cohesion, between autonomy and interdependence, and between discipline and serendipity. We have agreed that these are intrinsic in the volatile world of the clever team. None of these challenges occur within a vacuum. And from the moment that you start locating clever teams in the wider organizational context, you are forced to address the question, "What are the key characteristics of the clever organization, and how should leaders behave in them?" This is the focus of the last part of the book.

PART THREE

CLEVER ORGANIZATIONS

5 CONTOURS OF THE CLEVER ORGANIZATION

ORGANIZATIONS ARE broad churches. Their communities are diverse.

Take an organization like Cisco Systems, for example. It is brimming with clever yet highly diverse people. No two are the same—or want exactly the same relationship with the organization. Consider the following three Cisco employees.

Andreas Dohmen is a German nuclear physicist who also has a degree in economics. In his spare time he plays soccer and reads philosophy. "One day, I will study philosophy. That's my personal dream," he told us. His first job after university was as a system engineer and product manager at the German electronics giant Siemens. "I wanted to learn how a company works. I was fascinated by a company like Siemens, with 400,000 employees doing hundreds of millions of things and needing to make a lot of money every day. I wondered how this works in such a large organization. I wanted to learn."

It is typical of the way Dohmen thinks. "I like to solve problems," he says. "It sounds a bit odd, but I like to solve problems with people. It's my physics background. I like to stand in front of complex things and solve them. I strongly believe that the future lies in being cross-functional. Leadership has to do with how we develop more and more leaders who are capable of looking horizontally rather than just vertically."

Andreas Dohmen joined Cisco in 2001. "A lot of people mix it up and they say, we are Cisco, we are a start-up. I say, no, hold on, hundreds of millions of products every year don't ship with a start-up mentality. Forget it. You would screw up our partners and customers big-time if you thought like that. But at the same time, that should not make you an old economy company where processes beat innovation. The art is to keep both sides going at the same time. Be rigid, stick to it, but on the other side still have out-of-the-box thinking."

Then there is Christina Kite. When we met her, she was in Bangalore, India, overseeing a forty-five-day assignment as part of her responsibility for Cisco's real estate. "I have no real estate background at all, and I'm managing a $5 billion real estate portfolio. We have explosive growth in India, in Shanghai; we just put up new buildings in North Carolina and Atlanta. We're expanding in San Jose. It's a big role—like building a 3.5-million-square-foot campus. There are probably real estate execs that have lost their jobs trying to do that, seasoned execs with twenty-five-plus years of real estate experience!" Kite pauses for breath and then continues:

> I think what's very good about Cisco is, they are willing to take risks and to bet on the person, not necessarily whether the person has all the skills and the subject matter expertise or the technical knowledge. So I now have a background in risk and one in real estate.
>
> Just when I feel that I'm getting bored or going on autopilot, they throw another challenge in my direction. I've never had to go to them and say, I want this or I think I should

have that. It's almost like magically they seem to read my mind or are very observant. They've always challenged me. I'm not sure I can say I'm successful, because I always feel there's that higher bar.

Cisco is also the organizational home of Mark de Simone. "I've been in technology and management all my life," he told us. "I was fascinated with technology to begin with thirty years ago." Italian-born de Simone is vice president for Cisco's operations in the Middle East and Africa. He is responsible for Cisco's business in eighty-four countries and Cisco operations and offices in more than fifteen countries. He says:

> We are all unhappy with the status quo because we all know that there is a place, a thing, that the company, that we, that our teams, and individual contributors can do better. And this goes all the way down and, more importantly, across the organization. There is no one place where new great ideas come from. They come from everywhere. And if you allow people to experiment, and to make mistakes, and to learn, and to push the boundaries, you're going to have a true learning organization.
>
> Eventually, I think there will be this atomic principle: value will be about aggregating people who have a common interest and an idea, who are working on something together, who need to come together. And then they need to deliver that value, and, in time, these value chains are reabsorbed in other places.
>
> Companies will have to find a way to leverage this value, be able to evaluate it, and be able to support it with resources, and then eventually take away the resources so that other value can be created. This is the hardest thing to do for companies that come from the industrial era which emerged from Taylorism, specialization, the division of labor, and processes and systems that were repetitive and replicable.

Even at Cisco, we have replicable models. Why? A replicable model is a good thing because then you know its future. The only thing that is better than a replicable model is an adaptive replicable model, one which adapts continuously.

Andreas Dohmen. Christina Kite. Mark de Simone. Three very different people. All clever. All part of Cisco. Their stories are engagingly authentic. Andreas Dohmen, a philosophical soccer player (like Camus, one of his heroes); Christina Kite, a peripatetic real estate executive; and Mark de Simone, a visionary for a new kind of organization. Very different people with decidedly different experiences and views of life, linked by finding their organization—one with sixty three thousand other employees—a rewarding place to work.

This is the great challenge for modern organizations such as Cisco. And it isn't just high-tech companies that have to accommodate a diversity of intellects and interests; it is all organizations.

How every person within them relates to the organization is likely to be different. But somehow, they hold together.

How does Cisco do this? How can it offer a psychologically rewarding experience for three such different individuals? Part of the answer is that it recognizes and values just such diversity. It is large but feels small. It still smells like a start-up. It's been around but still feels new. It's exciting and edgy.

Large organizations have received bad press over recent years. The fashionable wisdom is that life is more fulfilling outside of an organization, somewhere where the individual has control of their destiny. The reality, however, is that the free-agent nation, described by Dan Pink and others, is the preserve of a minority—undoubtedly a substantial and important number, but a minority nevertheless.[1]

And even for this minority, it is not entirely clear that the benefits of liberation from organizational employment outweigh the costs. Stephen Barley and Gideon Kunda's ethnography of "itinerant experts" in the knowledge economy concludes, "During their more optimistic moments, contractors thought they had come close to achieving the American dream . . . They no longer had to conform to the whims of managers who once controlled their fate, and within reason they could speak their minds while focusing more exclusively on the technical aspects of their work."[2]

But there were caveats to this rosy picture of free-agent nirvana. Although they were no longer imprisoned in an "iron cage of bureaucracy," they found themselves suspended in webs of dependency that were no less constraining. Free agency and self-reliance did not mean freedom from social constraints or absence of reliance on others; it simply meant that the contractors' social dependencies had changed context.

So for better or for worse, most of the clever people at work in the clever economy work within (or are linked to) organizations, often extremely large organizations.

Remember that clever people *really* need organizations—to fund their dreams, to provide them with resources and a platform, and often, in a more basic way, to complement their skills and knowledge. As one of our interviewees bluntly put it, "There are all these clever people, but they're not quite as clever as they think they are, and while they would like to think that they're Nobel laureates and all the rest of it, some of them couldn't boil an egg."

As we have seen, there are tensions within this arrangement. Clever people have a history of uneasy relationships with organizations.

The individual craves independence. But the leader craves interdependence. This creates tension—tension that is intrinsic to the clever organization.

BEWARE: FRAGILE

But let's be clear: we are not organizational apologists. Organizations can and do go wrong. In the clever economy the balance is ever more precarious. At the extreme, if one person leaves, an organization can be rendered impotent. And when they go wrong, clever organizations can go wrong quickly.

As recent history has dramatically illustrated, there are many examples of organizations that have taken the speedy route to oblivion. Organizations can unravel with alarming rapidity.

We have seen banks, insurance companies, and car manufacturers reach bankruptcy with frightening speed. But remember, even before the dramas of 2008–2009, Arthur Andersen, perhaps the greatest professional services firm in the world, was destroyed in a month. Digital Equipment Corporation, which seemed destined to dominate the electronics market forever, was acquired by the new kid on the block, Compaq (dismissively described at the time as a mere box shifter). It doesn't matter how long-standing or august the organization: they are all fragile.

And fragility isn't the sole preserve of corporations. One very successful university declined rapidly after it appointed a diplomat to lead it. He didn't understand the academic world. "He stayed for five years and wouldn't go away," one disgruntled academic complained. "People in my own discipline fled. The great schools of the university just began to disintegrate. And it was all because he was somebody who they clearly didn't respect. There were little critical giveaways. Every Christmas card that came from the university during that period had the vice-chancellor on it— on a boat or planting a tree—but always there was a photograph of the vice-chancellor. Cynical as hell."

People as well as organizations are fragile. As we have seen, clever people need to be handled with care. The corollary of this is that they can become demotivated very quickly, and demotivated people destroy organizations as surely as problematic cash flow.

This is exacerbated in the contemporary organizational world, where the psychological contract is fragile, labor is highly mobile, reputations are more transient and open to undermining than ever before, and all of this takes place in a generally more complex and unstable environment.

HANDLE WITH CARE

Fred Hilmer, now the vice-chancellor of the University of New South Wales, has had to face this fragility in three very different organizational contexts: heading up McKinsey's Australasian practice, as boss of publishing giant Fairfax, and now in a university leadership role. He has been brought in to lead clever consultants, academics, and journalists—and always in challenging circumstances, where his no-nonsense, straightforward style of management has brought him both admirers and critics.

"When I took on the McKinsey job," Hilmer says, "the question was, should we keep the practice in Southeast Asia. At Fairfax there had been ten bosses in ten years—there was a flagging newspaper and a diminished company. Now as VC at the University of New South Wales, a central challenge is to articulate more demanding standards for faculty, staff, and students."

Hilmer draws strong contrasts between these organizational settings: "At McKinsey we could recruit to a culture—we looked for a strong fit and for loyalty. But journalists are different—they want to follow stories and get famous for it. For them, Fairfax (owners of the *Sydney Morning Herald*) was just a route. And in universities there is more competition; individuals want to get published to get better offers from other universities and leave—the loyalty factor is lower. With journalists and academics, the challenge is not to manage but to direct output—often by engaging directly in the writing or teaching process itself."

This type of direct engagement in the task is a way of gaining legitimacy, he says—another fragile commodity, as he learned to his cost. Hilmer is infamously remembered by journalists for his description of them as "content providers" and for his admission that he was "not an avid reader of newspapers."

"It was the truth, but I was foolishly honest," Hilmer conceded when we brought up the description in our conversations. "'Content provider' was a term I learnt to avoid because it was perceived as denigrating the craft of writing."

Despite the contrasts, Hilmer is adamant that the way things go rapidly wrong in these organizations is similar: "It's down to three things: the quality of leadership, the quality of the strategy, and bad appointments. One bad assignment in a consulting company, and the phone stops ringing. One bad story in a newspaper, and you lose a reader. One bad appointment in a university, and a whole department can be jeopardized."

RICH ORGANIZATIONS

With these dangers in mind, we have become keen observers of organizations. As we interviewed more and more clever people and their leaders, we were intrigued by how the organizations they worked in were coping. We looked for the fault lines, but we also looked for what held them together.

We found organizational richness in many places. The United Kingdom's National Health Service (NHS), for example, is one of the largest employers in the world; with 1.3 million employees, depending on which expert you believe, it is only outstripped by the U.S. Department of Defense, Wal-Mart, the Chinese army, and Indian Railways. Its budget is a massive £104 billion (more than $150 billion at current exchange rates). In recent years its CEO, David Nicholson, has turned a half-billion-pound deficit into a half-billion-pound credit. Patients report major improvements, but surveys still indicate that NHS staff and the general public do not. For David Nicholson, the greatest leadership challenge is winning the engagement of skeptical staff and the public.

From the NHS, we met a former nurse and former field hockey international player, Mary Edwards, now chief executive of the Basingstoke and North Hampshire NHS Foundation Trust. She is on the front line of delivering first-class health care. Her medical and managerial colleagues have cleverness in their DNA. One side effect of this particular phenomenon is that they all tend to believe that they are right most of the time. The challenges are huge, but you cannot fail to be invigorated when Edwards tells you how she tackles problems and opportunities. "People really do need direction, not management," she reflects. "It's exciting and intellectually stimulating." She is passionate about leadership and its consequences for delivering the kind of health care that transforms lives.

We also talked with neurosurgeon-turned-leader Peter Lees, a forthright and passionate advocate of leadership. He introduces himself by explaining that he takes "bits of people's brains out through their nose." In other words, he's an expert on pituitary cancer. "I don't now go into a room, and say to people, I'm a neurosurgeon who just happens to do a bit of leadership. I usually don't admit the neurosurgery bit. But I do sneak it into conversation every so often, if it looks like it would help. Sometimes, people just think you're a man in a gray suit, and you're some leadership guru—or not. Then you slip in, 'When I was medical director, I would never have done this.'" Peter is a source of much wisdom on the issue of leading clever people, not least his authorship of the marvelous, already quoted phrase "Leadership saves lives"; but he also recognizes that in the clever organizations he inhabits, leadership is at its most effective when it's invisible.

And we interviewed Jane Collins, chief executive of the world-renowned children's hospital at Great Ormond Street. Collins is a highly gifted pediatric neurologist with a straight-talking style but a wonderful warmth with her patients. "It is quite an isolated role and you have to enjoy that. Having a medical background does give you a certain something. I'm not saying that all chief execs of hospitals ought to be medically qualified. But understanding what it is that makes people tick, I think is important." She exemplifies two fundamental points about leading in the clever organization.

First, her medical background gives her legitimacy in this context, where knowledge and reputation mean a lot. Second, she understands that without human insight, her legitimacy means nothing.

In case you think that these examples are just about the United Kingdom, in response to the 2007 publication of the *Harvard Business Review* article that ignited this research project, the biggest group among the hundreds of e-mail responses came from senior hospital administrators all over the world. They shared the same concerns as Nicholson, Collins, Lees, and Edwards.

ATOMIC BOOSTER

As Collins says, understanding what makes people tick—especially clever people—is not just important; it is absolutely fundamental to clever organizations. As the Cisco examples at the start of this chapter illustrate, clever people are a hugely diverse bunch. No two clevers are the same. What organizations must do is, discover what they have in common, and focus their attention on achieving their joint objectives.

Of course, in some ways this is just a restatement of the fundamental issue of developing effective organizations. There are, in essence, only two problems in organizations: how to divide things up, thereby ensuring that the right people do the most appropriate work; and how to integrate the tasks of diverse individuals, functions, and teams to ensure that the organization gets things done.

Cisco's Mark de Simone talks about an "atomic principle." Value, he says, lies with organizations aggregating people who have a common interest and an idea—people who are working on something together, who need to come together. De Simone describes them as "value chains." It is a good phrase. His fascinating insight into the new world of organizations is that these value chains often extend beyond the boundaries of the organization. We are left with the tantalizing challenge that perhaps we need a fresh theory of the firm that can grasp new levels of complexity.

More prosaically, we can simply observe that these value chains are found in a wide variety of organizations. When we began this research, we thought that our case study material would come from the typical "knowledge economy" organizations: high-tech software firms, consultancies, sophisticated investment banks, and so on. But instead, we found cleverness in unexpected places.

Of course, organizational context still matters, but clever people are increasingly omnipresent in organizational life and, especially, at the heart of value creation.

For shorthand purposes, we categorize organizations into three general types:

- **Clever Inc.:** Largely concerned with the manufacture and distribution of standardized products

- **Clever Services:** As much as possible, primarily focused on the provision of standardized (albeit complex) services

- **Clever Collectives:** Typically dedicated to the creation of unique solutions involving both products and services

Let's examine each in turn and see the dynamics—and tensions—each produces.

CLEVER INC.

Werner Bauer, chief technology officer of Nestlé, identifies seven key elements to his job:

> My priority number one is to contribute to and accelerate Nestlé's transformation into a nutrition, health, and wellness company. This has to be substantiated by the right science.
>
> The second is to strengthen Nestlé's open innovation culture and create the base for disruptive innovation. Both are necessary. Normally, in a company where everything is very business oriented, disruptive innovation has no place. As

chief technology officer, I feel I have freedom to push disruptive innovation through.

The third point is about people: to recruit and develop people passionate about innovation and able to bridge R&D with operations and the commercial side. This bridging function always recurs because I don't believe in stand-alone R&D ideas.

The fourth is about performance culture: develop an outstanding R&D performance culture. That's really about how to support the performance culture. This is about systems and people management.

The fifth point is about going out, developing and sourcing core scientific and technological know-how, and driving science and technology platforms across all our business. This is about knowledge networks. I'm a strong believer of managing know-how by people and not by systems.

Sixth is to design our product systems and processes for inbuilt quality and safety. If you don't do it on the innovation side, you punish the other side.

And then the seventh one is to organize specific support and expertise and so on. This is about giving help to the operational side.

Few people we interviewed had their role so commendably clear in their mind as Werner Bauer. Others we talked with at Nestlé were also crystal-clear in their view of their roles, their place in the organization, and what it took to succeed. M&A specialist Jim Singh was clinically forthright in his assessment of how to succeed in the company: "We're good and we do good work, but there are a lot of people in the company that are equally good and do a hell of a lot of good work too. If you can get intelligence and competence and teamwork working together, then you will have a very rich career with the company. I am not shy in telling people you have to prove that you can work in different fronts, with different contexts and with different people. If not, you've got to look for somewhere else to build your career because you will not get my support." We asked Singh whether he had ever contemplated working in the lucrative investment banking industry. "My job is quite fulfilling. I would not survive in investment banking because I tend to be more strategic and less operational. I don't believe in spending my days and nights preparing blue books and running the clients. I tend to be more organized and a little more structured," he replied.

Both of these impressive executives illustrate the principle that in Clever Inc. clarity and organization matter. It is important to be clear about your priorities and efficient in delivering objectives. They come close to exemplifying the core competences of Clever Inc.

Nestlé is a traditional company proud of its heritage and keenly aware of its untouchables: those aspects of the business that should never change. And for this it cannot be criticized: it is a hugely successful company (the world's largest food company operating in every country on earth, selling thousands of products, and with revenues in excess of $79.8 million and profits of some $7.3 million). It has the structures and internal processes—and intellectual horsepower—to handle massive deals and product rollouts. Built on efficiency and economies of scale, it is typical of the type of organization that we call Clever Inc. Such organizations include fast moving consumer goods (FMCG) companies, but also industrial companies, such as car manufacturers and conglomerates.

In fact, most organizations that produce products fall into the category of Clever Inc. Indeed, the growth of the knowledge economy has sometimes led us to forget that not all clevers are located in organizations primarily involved in the creation, development, and transfer of specialist, intangible services: consultancies and professional firms, investment banks, research agencies, and so on. Many experts like Werner Bauer (a former university professor) work *within* manufacturing firms, while others make their clever contributions from managerial or operational line positions. Since we spoke with him, for example, Jim Singh has moved up from his M&A role at Nestlé to become finance director on the executive committee. It is easy to forget in the hype of the knowledge economy that manufacturing giants like Boeing, Lockheed Martin, and Toyota are also full of clever people.

LEARNING TO FORGET

But the challenges for Clever Inc. are those associated with moving from the dominant economic model of the twentieth century—efficiency through scale—to the dominant economic imperative of the twenty-first century: the ability to leverage knowledge. In particular, Clever Inc. must unlearn some habits that have served it well in the past.

The first of these is the tendency to process people. (And a company like Nestlé has a lot of people: over 265,000 employees.) By this we mean the overreliance on systemizing in order to scale up efficiencies. In the past, this allowed Clever Inc. to homogenize its workforce. This was more efficient as it meant that people could be relied upon to fit anywhere in the organization. "Corporate man" was the result, a suit-wearing bureaucrat whose loyalty to the organization was seemingly absolute. Over time, differences between employees were reduced, so that they provided a uniform input. They were steady and reliable. Indeed, for these traditional organizations, diversity is usually regarded as a problem. It leads to uncertain outcomes.

The ideological origins of Clever Inc. can be traced back to Frederick Taylor and the development of scientific management early in the twentieth century. Taylor's fundamental proposition was that work could be divided into two types: first, the labor of conception—thinking, which was to be concentrated in the hands of management; second, the labor of execution—doing, which was to be the domain of the worker. Taylor's thinking was groundbreaking and deeply rooted in its time. It effectively dominated ideas about organization for much of the twentieth century. It has given us time and motion studies, Gantt charts, work study, assembly lines, and all the paraphernalia of what passed for modern management for much of the last one hundred years.

Associated with scientific management was the tendency to progressively deskill work. It broke tasks down into the constituent parts, and then the manager stood by, stopwatch in hand, as the task was completed. In the fledgling years of mass manufacturing, scientific management ensured that Model Ts rolled effortlessly off production lines at Ford's Highland Park plant. But such ideas are anathema to the clever economy. In the clever economy, competitive advantage lies not with deskilling, but in investing in individuals with unique skills combining to deliver exceptional value to the organization.

"At its essence, 'modern' management is nothing more than a technology for 'getting more out of people,'" observes our colleague Gary Hamel. "Unfortunately, it's easy to lose sight of this simple truth when one is surrounded by the clanging, Rube Goldberg–like machinery of corporate decision-making—the never-ending budget wrangles, the elaborately staged planning sessions, the carefully scripted review meetings, and a gaggle of other similarly contentious and time-consuming rituals."[3] Sound familiar?

SAME OLD

The tendency to process people is linked with the second problem for Clever Inc. These organizations are addicted to efficiency. Traditionally, their ability to survive and beat the competition has been based on relentlessly ratcheting up efficiency. The organization's success depended on the ability to keep getting better at what it already does. The problem for Clever Inc. is that it is built to continue doing the same thing; but it is less good at identifying new things that it should be doing.

We see this issue writ large in the modern-day preoccupations of large corporations: how can we get better at innovation? It is found in the obsession of pharmaceutical companies that almost always think of innovation as a new drug; in banks seeking new, complex products; in FMCG companies in their search for new flavors and colors. Innovation is the organizational drug of choice. There is another element to this: how can large, sprawling organizations replicate the entrepreneurial culture of a start-up? How can they be big while feeling small? How can they enjoy the scope and size of the giant corporation *and* the agility of the entrepreneurial start-up?

The third problem with Clever Inc. is what Karl Marx called alienation. He believed that the division of labor—associated with the application of scientific management—deprived individuals of a sense of achievement. Deskilled meant deprived. Working on an assembly line, simply performing the same routine task again and again, workers were separated from both the act of creation and the product of their labor. This is not a historical detail—ask someone who works in a call center. Indeed, the current obsession with employee engagement is symptomatic of continuing alienation for many millions in the working population.[4]

CLEVER EVOLUTION

Clearly, Clever Inc.'s capacity to homogenize human talent, its preoccupation with incremental improvement and frequent lack of human fulfillment, sits uneasily with maximizing clever people and clever teams. And yet, it would be premature to sound the death knell for Clever Inc.

Nestlé provides a powerful case for the enduring nature of Clever Inc. It is a huge organization, yet it has been able to change and continually innovate. Before the Internet was fully established, for example, the company led the establishment of virtual shopping through interactive television; it was a pioneer in business-to-business (B2B) commerce; and its Globe project involved the implementation of one of the world's most ambitious data management and corporate information systems. Its recent introduction of Nespresso has enabled a sea change in consumer expectations of easily producible, high-quality espresso coffee—successfully deploying new technology, alternative channels of distribution, and innovative promotion (meaning George Clooney ads). Perhaps most radical of all is Nestlé's overall ambition to transform itself from a food company to a nutrition, health, and wellness business.

This achievement is based on an important recognition of its own strengths and weaknesses. The high-caliber people at Nestlé, as we have seen, tend to have a crystal-clear view of how and where they create value. More broadly, what Clever Inc. is good at is taking a new innovation and rapidly scaling it up, or commercializing it. Scale is what Clever Inc. brings to the clever economy, and, unquestionably, scale still counts.

In their book *Fast Second*, our colleagues Costas Markides and the late Paul Geroski argue that instead of trying to behave like highly innovative start-ups, large organizations would be better advised to concentrate on what they are good at. "Big established firms should leave the task of creation to the market—the thousands of small, start-up firms around the world that have the requisite skills and attitudes to succeed at this game," advise Markides and Geroski. "Established firms should, instead, concentrate on what they are good at—which is to consolidate young markets into big mass markets."[5]

This requires organizations that can create what we call an ecology of start-ups around themselves. This is true for pharmaceutical companies that increasingly license-in compounds from small research organizations, and for giant record companies that handle the sales and marketing for small, passionate niche players. Innovative ideas are taken in and subjected to the discipline and efficiency of Clever Inc.

Of course, it would be naive and simplistic to imagine that breakthrough innovation does not take place inside Clever Inc. It does. For example, Unilever dreamed up the idea of repositioning a margarine—Flora—as a health food. If you ask an employee what business they are in at Flora, they will tell you they are in the healthy hearts business. Rather, what we are suggesting is that Clever Inc. continues to use its expertise at scaling up products and markets while seeking clever innovation from wherever it can find it—inside or outside the organizations. Witness the interest in open innovation, for example, among companies such as Procter & Gamble.

There is also another route for Clever Inc. IBM was a manufacturer of hardware until changes in its market forced it to evolve. In keeping with Clever Inc.'s difficulty with recognizing big innovations, Big Blue failed to recognize the sea change in the computing world with the advent of the PC. Rather than make the switch to software—where the new value lay—it famously persisted in doing what it had always done. Over time, the hardware became a commodity—squeezing margins and forcing less efficient players out of the market. IBM was in danger of sleepwalking off a cliff. But galvanized by massive losses and the arrival of new leadership in the guise of Louis Gerstner as CEO, the company transformed itself from a hardware manufacturer into a service solutions company. Big Blue evolved from Clever Inc. into a clever services organization.

The lesson from IBM is that Clever Inc. can and must evolve. To do so does not require that it turn itself into a funky start-up—that would be as farcical as it is uncommercial. But Clever Inc. can learn to thrive in the twenty-first century by reconnecting with what made it great in the first place. Nestlé realizes that its strength lies in scaling up. IBM realized that it had become complacent and had lost touch with its consumers and how it could add value.

CLEVER SERVICES

The second general organizational type is what we call Clever Services. This is where organizations are focused on the provision of standardized—but complex—services. Historically, these organizations were built around highly credentialed professional groups—law, accounting, and medicine, for example—but more recent additions include advertising, PR, and consulting.

Clever Services are where concentrated numbers of specialized or expert clevers first emerged in large, increasingly globalized firms. The managerial challenges of Clever Services are familiar. They include controlling standards and performance levels of separate and distinct professional groups; coordinating individuals who value high levels of autonomy; exercising control within typically loose, decentralized structures; and building organizational and leadership skills among staff whose primary orientation is toward their professional peers and their shared expertise.[6]

Among the Clever Services included in our research—accounting and legal firms, investment banks, consultants, media services, and so on—three issues stand out.

The first of these is the problem of retaining their clever people. What has traditionally happened with Clever Services organizations is that people stay long enough to become qualified and then they leave. This is a classic problem for accounting and legal practices, compounded by the way the partner structure operates.

What often happens is that the elite firms, like Pricewaterhouse-Coopers (PwC), which recruit very bright young people from the best universities, find it hard to deliver on the expectations they have created through the recruitment process. If these firms are not careful, the best and brightest quickly perceive that the road to partnership is tough, long, and uncertain. They may be tempted to leave as soon as they have qualified—going either into industry or to the tempting attractions of investment banking or consulting.

When we examine the aggregate retention rates for such firms, the numbers look satisfactory. But the key challenge is retaining the best. There are, of course, steps that these organizations, like PwC, can take to address this issue.

For example, PwC has an important initiative around making sure that the first five years are rewarding for its bright graduate recruits. There is a drive to offer early experience of leadership by breaking down complex projects into smaller pieces and allowing relatively junior staff to take lead roles. This is combined with the use of mentoring systems that allow for a degree of organizational control without overly constraining talented individuals. In addition, rotation around various parts of the practice—tax, audit, consulting, business recovery, transaction services—sustains interest and gives junior staff an overall view of the business. For organizations such as PwC, addressing the retention issues is not just about cost control but is much more about securing a future talent stream.

Problems arise if talented recruits are left doing what they regard as—and what may well be—grunt work for too long. If this is allowed to happen, many will elect to gain their professional qualifications and leave.

The second problem with Clever Services organizations is that they encourage overspecialization. By their very nature, they require deep expertise. We would find this in law firms like Linklaters (one of the "magic circle" firms in the City of London) and in the Big Four accounting firms—PwC, KPMG, Deloitte, and Ernst & Young—as well as specialized market research organizations, like Kantar. It is imperative to develop individuals who can offer cutting-edge expertise. There is a sense in which these organizations are fundamentally in the knowledge business. The danger is that excessive specialization both lowers morale and in the longer term limits the extent to which skilled practitioners can offer complex solutions that integrate knowledge from several areas. For the professional services firms, this manifests itself in an inability to offer services that cross the lines of the specialties. As clients present ever more complex problems, this ability to combine knowledge bases is becoming more significant. Viewed from the perspective of the individual, the prospect of developing deep expertise in a technical area for up to ten years before partnership becomes a realistic prospect is an unattractive psychological contract.

The third issue for Clever Services is one that we touched on in an earlier chapter: the fact that clever professionals identify with their profession rather than the organization (or its customers). A brain surgeon identifies with other specialist brain surgeons rather than his or her medical colleagues—be they nurses, cleaners, or even other surgeons—at any particular hospital. Their professional affiliation is also stronger than their association with patients. The challenge for Clever Services is to nurture collective identification among individualistic professionals—be they doctors, lawyers, accountants, teachers, or business school professors.

At the British Broadcasting Corporation (BBC), talented program makers identify with other program makers whether they are in the organization or not. Indeed, their sense of identity derives from membership in a group that extends beyond the organization. They are especially sensitive to recognition from outside. Working in television in the United Kingdom, where the most prestigious awards are the BAFTAs, awarded by the British Academy of Film and Television Arts, we have heard people introduce themselves just like this: "Hi, I am Helen—two BAFTAs." As if that's all you needed to know about them.

To address these issues, the BBC began a culture change program called Building One BBC, which encouraged an identification with the whole organization and fostered cooperation between different media: TV, radio and online. To combat overspecialization, the BBC developed an extensive "attachment scheme," which allowed people to experiment in another area of expertise, so that seasoned children's TV program makers could try their hand at serious documentaries—often with innovative results.

CLEVER COLLECTIVES

The third type of clever organization we identify is one we call Clever Collectives. These are much more freewheeling organizations, built on know-how rather than the efficiencies of Clever Inc., and on networks rather than the hierarchies of Clever Services organizations. Examples of Clever Collectives include Google, Microsoft, and Arup. You will also find Clever Collectives buried within more established organizations as diverse as Johnson & Johnson (J&J), Roche, and Oracle.

In many ways, the Clever Collectives are the best suited to our times. This is not surprising, as many of these organizations have grown up in the clever economy.

Take Google, for example. As everyone now knows, the company was founded in 1998 by Sergey Brin and Larry Page. The mathematical analysis behind the search engine is dazzling, as you might expect from two very clever mathematicians. Page was born to be a computer programmer—his father was a computer science professor. He earned a science and engineering bachelor's degree at the University of Michigan and then started a PhD at Stanford University. Brin, who hails from Moscow, graduated with a bachelor of science degree in mathematics and computer science from the University of Maryland at College Park. His knowledge of data extraction and search engine technology is legendary.

Brin and Page met at Stanford as PhD students in computer science. By their own accounts, they didn't hit it off right away. They have been reported as saying they found each other obnoxious (typical clevers!). But their mutual love of technology and the need to collaborate overcame their dislike, and the two ended up working on a project conducting research into creating a better search engine. The project became part of their doctoral theses and then a major part of their lives. By mid-1998 the two had abandoned their doctorates. The rest, as they say, is corporate history.

The point about Google is that, like many other high-tech companies, it was started by clever techies. The name Google is itself an allusion that only clevers would understand. A googol represents a one followed by one hundred zeros. Brin and Page used the association with googol to suggest the mind-boggling amount of information available on the Internet. Even the name was intended to appeal to other clevers.

We visited the now famous corporate headquarters of Google in Silicon Valley. The site is alive with the buzzy social interactions of clever people. We met Carolyn Yates from the company's engineering training organization. When she joined Google four years previously, there were about one thousand employees. At the time we spoke, there were sixteen thousand. A lot has changed (at the time of writing there are now twenty thousand employees!)—but they try to keep the fundamentals the same. "We aim to offer people the freedom to be really good. I think that's what Google is really about: the freedom to do your best work. My job is to help make that happen," Yates explains.

In creating an organization, Page and Brin were also acutely aware of the importance of values and meaning. Google's slogan is "Do no evil," a phrase that resonates for its clever employees.

Going forward, we believe that Google and other Clever Collectives face a number of distinct organizational challenges. The first is that the very source of organizational strength—their mission—can become a cultural straitjacket. Over time, organizations need space to adapt to their changing circumstances. The worry for an organization like Google is that the beliefs of the founding fathers can easily become a cult. Over time, what started out as a simple philosophy can become a rigid doctrine or ideology that is resistant to new ideas and ways of looking at the world. This can lead to cultural and organizational sclerosis. In the end, insiders may become hostile to anyone from outside who challenges the beliefs of the cult. What began as intellectual curiosity and good intentions can easily become dogma.

A second potential danger for Clever Collectives is that they become divided into a number of different groups. Whereas in the first scenario they are united behind a single immutable set of beliefs, in this scenario the organization fragments, with different parts adhering to their own set of beliefs or view of the world. So, for example, in the case of Google, the people designing search software may regard their mission as fundamentally different from—and even at odds with—the people selling online advertising. Such differences are often most obvious when companies grow through acquisition. Merger integration is notoriously difficult to achieve. When Clever Collectives combine, the challenges are likely to be even greater.

While we were writing, for example, Microsoft—another Clever Collective—launched a massive bid to acquire Yahoo!, another search company. Regardless of the financial and strategic implications of such a deal, the organizational challenges of combining two very different clever cultures would be immense. The danger with fragmentation is that part or all of the organization loses its identity and becomes a captive culture. This sort of organizational colonialism is not well suited to the clever economy. The danger for Microsoft is that the really clever people at Yahoo! might leave to join Google—adding to the competitive pressures Microsoft is trying to combat.

How might the new generation of Clever Collectives deal with these twin challenges of rigid adherence to ideology on the one hand (overintegration) and organizational colonialism (as a response to disintegration) on the other? There are some lessons to be learned from a previous generation of clever organizations.

Johnson & Johnson, for example, is well known for its strong values and overarching culture—best captured in the legendary J&J credo. But what helped to give the company its longevity is a continual questioning of the credo—through workshops, training programs, projects, and so on—which gives the credo a living, vibrant presence that must be actively applied to new challenges and contexts. The complacency of the cult is avoided.

In a related sector, Roche, the Swiss pharmaceutical business, has learned the value of deliberately resisting excessive corporate control (colonialism) as it has grown through acquisition. For example, Roche limited its ownership of the Japanese pharmaceutical company Chugai to 51 percent in an effort to preserve Chugai's culture and individuality. Maintaining that diversity is Roche's most challenging task—for the pressures to unify and centrally direct are huge. Witness its recent attempt to take full ownership of biotech firm Genentech.

COLLECTIVE COMPLEXITY

The final challenge for Clever Collectives is creating an organizational form that can cope with the complexity that comes with scale. In truth, this is the issue behind the previous two dangers as well. Clever Inc., as we have seen, was predicated on efficiencies of scale. Traditionally, it dealt with complexity by homogenizing its inputs: people, processes, and products. Clever Collectives, however, are not built on efficiencies of size. In fact, they are built on the opposite: economies of clever. For them, homogenization is not an option. Efficiency is not the basis of their success, and command and control is anathema to how they function.

As Tristram Carfrae at Arup vigorously expresses it, "Clever people are not bloody rats that you stick in cages, and you—Mr. Manager—walk up and down in the middle and somehow make them do something. That's not how it works. How do you lead people who don't want to be managed? That's the question. People may object to *who* the leader is, but they *do* want leadership from someone they respect."

As an organization, Arup may not be that "efficient." Carfrae describes it as "very organic, very chaotic . . . Incredibly hard to swing the firm in a violent way. Every individual has the right of self-determination. To move them, you have to persuade them, every single one of them, that this is a good thing for their firm to be doing—and good for them. It is *incredibly* time consuming and *incredibly* frustrating. But it's a great strength!"

The competitive advantage of Clever Collectives is built on diversity of perspective and autonomy, and their modus operandi is collaboration. As they grow larger, they must find alternative structures and strategies for coping with the increasing complexity.

We have already addressed the dangers of one possible solution: adherence to a single rigid ideology. The danger here is in becoming a cult. And we have also highlighted the risk of fragmentation if the organization fails to find a way to glue itself together. In effect, these are the two extremes of centralization and decentralization.

The other traditional solution to complexity has been the development of a matrix structure. This is a hybrid of centralized and decentralized organization. In effect, the organization creates a complex structure to mirror its complex nature. But matrix structures rarely operate in quite the way they are planned. Balancing power between different functional, market, or geographical axes is always difficult, and ambiguity and conflict are built into the systems rather than eliminated. Many Clever Collectives now mix matrices with project structures, networks of subcontractors, and spin-offs variously engaged with consumers and customers in what is now referred to as "cocreation."

Today, even the discussion of the matrix organization can seem a bit old hat. Most organizations are now in some fuzzy, postmatrix phase, with projects, start-ups, networks of subcontractors, and so on. One organization grappling with these issues is Kantar, the global research and information consultancy. It is in the top three in its sector. Within the Kantar Group are well-known names such as Millward Brown, Research International, BMRB, and Added Value. Kantar operates not really as a matrix organization, but more as a series of independent companies loosely bound together by a manifesto of values, shared central services, and business development undertaken by a small group of people working for the group.

Lucy Gill is a group client director reporting directly to Kantar CEO Eric Salama. In her marketing career, she spent several years with Nestlé, before joining a global consulting firm in a management position. She entered the Kantar group in 2003, as a managing director for one of the smaller retail companies before becoming a director. She knows what it is like to lead in a more formal hierarchical setting—the difference, in effect, between Clever Inc. and Clever Collectives.

As we spoke to her, overlooking the blue waters of Sydney Harbor, she reflected on the challenges of trying to persuade the separate companies—local Clever Collectives, if you will—to collaborate to deliver. "I have no formal power and my mission is often blocked by individual accounting and reward systems which are locally driven—this is a huge challenge!" she says. "What's more, many of the research experts are not really corporately driven. Instead of tweaking a model and reselling it, they always want to start from scratch and make things perfect. This might make clever people cleverer, but it doesn't make us richer! Most of my persuasion is done via lots of travel and face-to-face time, doing lots of legwork and hand holding—I often feel like a PA."

Gill's current specialty is "shopper marketing" (targeting the behavior of the shopper, not the consumer) to look at who buys what in the supermarkets, why, and how. Her business development work in shopper marketing with major global clients is then used as a theme to focus the efforts of the separate Kantar businesses that need to collaborate to deliver.

So in managing the interfaces of a complex structure, Gill is back to some simple leadership basics: lots of face time and focus around buyer priorities.

CHAIN REACTIONS

There is no escaping the fact that the growth of the clever organization challenges many of our cherished assumptions about firms and the way they interact. The economic theory of the firm, a fundamental building block of managerial economics, sees firms as separate entities with clear and firm boundaries, competing in markets where there are clear winners and losers. But in the knowledge economy, the boundaries of organizations are increasingly fuzzy. In addition, complexity and dynamic change may make it essential to forge alliances with suppliers, customers, and even competitors. From the simple world of "I win, you lose," we have moved to the pursuit of win-win solutions. Large organizations, in particular, have found themselves forced to develop relationships with smaller, faster, smarter organizations in order to sustain rates of innovation. As Cisco's Mark de Simone observes, "Value chains increasingly extend beyond organizational boundaries. Companies will have to find a way to leverage this value, be able to evaluate it, and be able to support it with resources."

The most effective clever organizations will be collections of value networks—or, as noted in the last chapter, temporary value chains. These deliver a particular project or perform as a particular team and then, once they have completed their work, are reabsorbed in other places. This is precisely the challenge that Cisco has been handling and, as we saw at the beginning of this chapter, creating attractive places for clever people to express themselves.

The final chapter begins with an extract from our interview with the CEO of Google China, the archetypal "new" organization located in one of the economies that will dominate the twenty-first century. But as you read his fascinating insights into the challenges he and his organization face, you may recognize similar issues in unleashing the potential of your smartest people.

6 THE FUTURE OF CLEVER ORGANIZATIONS

WHAT WILL THE ORGANIZATIONS of the twenty-first century look like? The easy answer is that despite the traumas of the recent past, they will look very much like the organizations of the twentieth century. Organizations do not change overnight. But we believe that the years that follow will see subtle changes to the organizations that we know today. Not all organizations will change, of course. Some will remain obstinately the same. Over time, however, we believe those organizations will fade away. They will be overtaken and ultimately replaced by organizations that are fit for the new challenges of the clever economy.

In some organizations those changes are already taking place. Think of Google. Today it is the darling of the high-tech sector, much beloved of investors, users—and clever people. It may not always be so favored, but it has an important advantage over other organizations. The Internet-search company has benefited from being at the cutting edge of many of the developments that we

149

have described in the previous two parts. Google truly is a creature of the clever economy.

If we were to create our archetypal clever person from those we have encountered throughout the world, Kai-Fu Lee would probably be close. We met him in Beijing, where he heads Google's China operations. His résumé reads like a *Who's Who* of clever organizations. Prior to joining Google, he worked at Microsoft, where he was responsible for advanced natural language and user interface technologies. He also founded Microsoft Research Asia, which has since become one of the best research centers in the world. From 1996 to 1998, Lee was president of Cosmo Software, a subsidiary of Silicon Graphics Inc. (SGI). There, he was responsible for several product lines and the company's Web strategy. Before joining SGI, Lee spent six years at Apple Computer, most recently as vice president of the company's interactive media group, which developed multimedia technologies such as QuickTime. From 1988 to 1990, he was an assistant professor at Carnegie Mellon University, where he developed the world's first speaker-independent continuous speech-recognition system, selected as the "Most Important Innovation of 1988" by *BusinessWeek*. Along the way, he also developed a computer program to play the game *Othello*, which defeated the human world champion in 1988.

We wanted to talk to Lee about the shape of organizations to come. Google, after all, is a clever organization created by clever people for clever people. His thoughts are as fascinating as they are daunting. "The twentieth century was all about hardworking engineers," summarizes Kai-Fu Lee. "The twenty-first century is about flat organizations that must collaborate and compete."

PRAGMATIC ORGANIZATIONS

As we have seen, the people who work for the new organizations have different priorities and needs. The organizations, in turn, need different sorts of workers. According to Kai-Fu Lee, the new organizations of the twenty-first century first require what he describes as "innovative pragmatists."

Informed and innovative pragmatism is rife at Google. There are no research labs at Google. The company does not believe in the ivory tower approach. Great ideas do not emerge only from a handpicked elite. Rather, Google has democratized innovation. Everyone is equal. Scientists and engineers are equivalent. Google can be viewed as an organizational form that Henry Mintzberg describes as an "adhocracy." It is characterized by innovation all over.

To see how this works in practice, you only have to observe how it treats its employees—not just a chosen few but all its employees. Most obvious are the perks the company provides for staff. At Google's HQ, employees enjoy free meals at a selection of restaurants. Also on offer are massages, valet parking, and a hair salon. Every article written about Google rhapsodizes about the perks and benefits enjoyed by employees. Yet the corporate pampering is nothing more than enlightened self-interest. As Kai-Fu Lee points out, the company spends a mere $20 per day per employee on restaurants. It is actually a tiny amount compared with the organizational benefits. If you feed employees well, you remove one of the primary distractions in the working day. People who eat together stay together and feel good. They also collaborate more.

Kai-Fu Lee goes on to argue that the organization of the future needs to include not analysts but synthesizers. Clever organizations place a premium on the ability to synthesize multiple points of view. Analysis only gets you so far. In the end, the clever economy requires synthesis: a recombining of inputs to create something new and better.

ONLY SYNTHESIZE

The growing importance of synthesis is recognized in an exciting strand of the psychology literature. Renowned worldwide for his theory of multiple intelligences, Howard Gardner is professor of cognition and education at the Harvard Graduate School of Education. Moving on from his multiple-intelligence work, Gardner is now focusing on the future and "the cognitive abilities that will command a premium in the years ahead." In his book *Five Minds for the Future,* he offers an insight into the qualities of thinking that will allow people to survive and prosper in the twenty-first century, both in work and in life generally.

One of Gardner's five minds is what he calls "the synthesizing mind." As he explains, "The synthesizing mind stems from the fact that we all are deluged with information. How do you decide what to pay attention to, what to ignore, how to put it together in a way that makes sense to you? How do you communicate your synthesis to other people? That's probably the most distinctive mind, because I've given a label to something that people haven't really talked about much before."[1]

At Google, Kai-Fu Lee sees a similar process at work in the marketplace. "Look at the successful products of recent years. Apple's iPhone, for example, combines a cell phone with touch screen, an MP3 (iPod), Internet access, good software, and a good user interface. It is a triumph of synthesis, combining several existing functions into one sleek design." It is the ability to synthesize, Lee notes, that sets the new clevers apart. Or compare Google itself with the "father" of search engine offering LexisNexis access. LexisNexis offers deep, specialized search for particular domains, but Google's success is built on parallel algorithms, machine learning, web "crawlers," all running behind a superior user interface. It is *Google* that has entered the language of the twenty-first century as a verb.

Being smart is a start. But if you haven't got the necessary skills to collaborate, then chances are, you aren't going to create value for the organization in the clever economy. Pure academic intelligence (IQ) can be dangerous without a degree of emotional intelligence (EQ). Kai-Fu Lee notes that this is true even for Googlers. "Arrogant geniuses always backfire," he says. "They become a terror to other engineers. They may be a hundred times cleverer, but an arrogant genius can demoralize a thousand people."

The anomaly here is that Google's organization was actually inspired by an academic institution, and as we have pointed out, academics tend not to be great team players. Says Lee:

> Proper management at university is hands off, leave the professors, they are the experts, you are just the administrator. I think Google tries to emulate that model; increasingly obviously, we have to think about strategies and business competition. We built our model after the Stanford model, and we are quite proud of that. We try to steer toward hiring really smart people and let them decide what they want to do. It makes management more of a challenge because if you truly do that to the extreme, then what is the purpose of a university administrator? Just to get funding, to arrange the building and offices; that's a boring job, right? That's why you are writing and teaching rather than being a dean; you don't talk about innovation with the deans. At Google our VPs and directors are really smart people, too. Generally they will drive and own strategy prioritization, and some itch for technical work so [they] do it on the side. So if you look at our VPs, some are more administrative, some are more strategic, some are more technical. It's unclear which type will be the most successful—while you might place low odds with the administrators, don't forgot they might be the most empowering, and thus fit our model the best.

It has taken a commercial organization to make the academic organizational model work successfully.

THINK TO LEAD

Closely linked to the ability to collaborate is the need to communicate effectively. Clever people need to *think* to communicate.

Often, their level of specialist knowledge is such that their colleagues—and their leaders—find it difficult to understand what they are saying. Both clevers and their leaders have to think hard about the audience when they are communicating. This is especially challenging for leaders. As Google's Lee advises, "Lead, don't preach."

Communication is a massive issue for the organizations of the future. On the one hand, new technology means that we live in an era of instant messaging, but that also brings new perils. As organizations become more network based (rather than hierarchical), the need to have open dialog is more acute. At the same time, control becomes ever more problematic. Modern organizations are extremely porous to communication. An ill-judged e-mail can rapidly be circulated on the Internet, prompting blog entries and other unsolicited actions. Managing this in an open and transparent—and yet productive and sensible—way is something that organizations will have to come to grips with.

Passionate workers are also a notable characteristic of Google. In the past, a degree of enthusiasm—real or feigned—was considered perfectly adequate for most jobs. But in the clever economy, merely going through the motions is not enough. The organizations that thrive will be ones that harness the passion of their clever people. *Passion*, of course, is a word that makes people distinctly uncomfortable, especially in the context of work (we should know—we are British!). But in the future, the ability to create an organizational context where passion is the norm rather than the exception will be vital.

What Google has realized is that if you love your job, you are not working. But even within a passionate workforce, there may be telling variations. As Lee explains, the company hires many recent PhD students and postdoctoral students—but the PhD students typically outperform the others. Why? Lee believes that whereas the postdocs are allocated by others to work on projects, the PhD students can choose what they work on. Their free choice is linked with higher levels of personal commitment and perfor-mance. To this may be added responsibility. If you choose your project, you have a responsibility to make it work.

On the *Spore* team at Electronic Arts, some of the highest per-formers spend a considerable amount of their time, sometimes 20 or 25 percent, working at home. "When they need that time alone, when they're working on a really tough problem, they liter-ally don't come into the office," Will Wright explains, adding:

> They will take that time to focus—no phone, no interruptions. It's interesting because everybody in the office has that oppor-tunity, but it is invariably only the really highly functioning ones that take it. Most come into the office, put in their eight hours, and that's that. And then there are about five people on our team that will spend a significant amount of time working at home, and those are the ones that have the highest produc-tivity. I think that is almost an innate instinct these people al-ready have, and even if we didn't tell them that this is an opportunity, they would find a way to carve it out; they would lock their door and put up a 'do not disturb' sign or some-thing. They have clearly learned they need these blocks of alone time to do what they do. Their imagination is right at the limits. This is why they need to be left alone at times.

FREE TO DO

This is a theme that runs through the Google culture. The com-pany prides itself on letting people do their own thing. The com-pany encourages employees to act like internal entrepreneurs. But better still for clevers, Google has a very bottom-up approach to innovation. Great ideas can come from anywhere. When new ideas arise they are collected and ranked on the Google Top 100.

But of course this is not quite enough—people need time to de-velop and pursue their ideas. Central to the Google intrapreneurship approach is the concept of 20 percent time. It is the time given to people to work on whatever they want to. Employees spend one day a week developing start-up ideas known colloquially as Googlettes. Real innovation comes out of this process. For example, the social networking Web site Orkut started life as a Googlette.

Says Kai-Fu Lee:

> We want to attract great people, but we know great people want to be empowered; they want to do their thing. That's why we have this 20 percent time you've heard a lot about. We try to have loosely organized organizations where the span of control, which is how many people you manage, tends to be like twenty or forty or fifty. So it really over-whelms a manager or director who just manages people or writes reviews all day, so they hardly have time to tell people what to do. Having said that, I think people still find it more disciplined than they want. Our turnover tends to be very low, 2 percent worldwide, and the few people we lose tend to be those who have finally said, I am going to do my own thing; a few retire, but others go do that; that's true, I think, across the globe. We also manage, to my surprise, to keep a lot of these people by giving them the playground they want.

Of course, there are cultural differences that have an impact on Google's brand of proactive self-starters. Some cultures—the more individualistic cultures associated with the West—encourage individuals to take the initiative. Knowledge workers in North America and Western Europe, for example, are often more demanding and also more inclined to say what they think. In the clever economy, extracting ideas from the heads of the organization's people is an imperative. If those people are culturally disinclined to say what's on their mind, then this is more difficult.

At Google in China, employees were initially disbelieving of the concept of spending time on their own ideas. When Kai-Fu Lee hires Chinese graduates, they expect to receive orders. Even when they are told they can have time to spend on their projects, no one dares to. In response, Lee's team has set up processes to encourage people to use the freedom that is offered. They gather groups of around ten people together, invite them to brainstorm a particular issue, and see what are the best ideas that come out. Members of the group are then given a 20 percent project to create more confidence and comfort that they are not going to be punished. Lee even orchestrated a "20 percent time lecture" by a headquarters engineer. All the employees were asked to come to this lecture. The long-haired headquarters engineer started by saying, "All the managers, raise your hand." Then he said, "Please leave now." He then explained to all the engineers that the managers have no business in the engineers' 20 percent time.

Lee is also working hard at adapting his style. "When someone disagrees with me, I go out of my way to acknowledge and thank the person so that people see it is OK to disagree with me. Also we try not to create hierarchies in management, we try not to make distinctions between local employees and U.S. employees, and we create a work environment that is equal. My office is no larger than anyone else's. So we try all these things, and I think we are continually making progress toward people believing this is truly a Google culture. But I wouldn't say we are there yet."

There is something of the resilient optimist about Kai-Fu Lee. If he were asked, "Is the glass half full or half empty?" we know which side he would be on. That is a question that clever people always face. No matter what they have achieved so far, there is always more to be done. Remaining positive is an important component of any innovation culture. When he started teaching at Carnegie Mellon, for example, Lee received negative feedback from his students. A pessimist might have taken the negative comments as a sign that he was not cut out for the classroom. But he persisted and bounced back. Clever optimists regard adversity as an opportunity to improve, a challenge to be overcome. Organizations that encourage this attitude will prosper in the long run. For example, organizations that not only tolerate but positively celebrate failure are more likely to produce breakthrough innovation.

At the same time, organizations that enjoy a reputation for risk taking will attract risk takers. Talent attracts talent. As hire As, and Bs hire Cs.

Kai-Fu Lee's thoughts on the shaping of the twenty-first-century organization are primarily concerned with the sort of people who organizations require. It begs the question, What sort of organizations will attract and develop individuals with these sorts of characteristics? In other words, what do organizations need to do to make themselves fit for the clever economy?

The organizations of the future will have to adapt. If they don't, clever people will vote with their feet—and with their talents. As with evolution, the organizations that survive will be the ones best suited to the new environment.

We believe those questions relate to three important themes for holding clever organizations together: discipline, meaning, and interdependence.

PROVIDE CLEAR AND SIMPLE RULES

When we began our research into leading clever people, we wrote that a key attribute of clever leaders was that they protected their followers from organizational "rain." We have learned that this is necessary but insufficient. It's also important to minimize the chances that the rain will fall by creating an environment in which the organizational rules and norms are simple and universally accepted.

All organizations have rules, but clever people thrive under two particular circumstances. First, a relative absence of rules—that is to say, a few clear rules, which are universally enforced. They will react badly to the miasma of bureaucratic rules characteristic of many large organizations—despairing of the head office and its capacity to tie them down. Second, the rules need to be ones that they agree to—for example, safety rules in pharmaceutical companies, risk rules in banks, integrity rules in professional services firms. Sociologists call these *representative* rules, and they are the ones that clever people respond to best.

The distinction comes from the sociologist Alvin Gouldner, who argued that in traditional hierarchical organizations, the existence of rules gave the powerful two sources of power: the power to enforce the rules or the power to ignore them. In exchange for favors, rules can be ignored. This gives rise to what he calls "mock bureaucracy," a situation where there are a plethora of rules but one can never be certain of when they will be applied; and an "indulgency pattern," where individuals engage in the tacit exchange of favors in order to buy freedom from the rules.[2]

Both of these conditions are anathema to clever people. They favor no rules—so that they can express their unique skills. But organizations can't operate like this. As Dan Teodosiu at Microsoft observes, "Clever people can be sources of great ideas, but unless they have systems and discipline, they may deliver very little." Or as Sir Simon Rattle, the conductor of the legendary Berlin Philharmonic, puts it, "If I take too many decisions for them the plane never leaves the ground, but if I take none there is chaos."[3] So the task for clever organizations is to simplify the rule environment, removing as many petty restrictions as possible but insisting on a few rules, which come to have the force of law. Best of all is when these few rules can be consensually accepted. For example, coding rules at Microsoft—all of those who write code agree that these must be adhered to in order for everyone to thrive.

A small number of clear rules can set clever people free. Louise Makin notes, "We transformed things when we actually put just one or two very clear cross-company processes—for example, this is how we will make these investment decisions, and it will be this group of people."

Returning to an earlier point, clearly a major benefit of having a few simple rules is that it will allow individuals the space to take risks and possibly fail.

This is how Fujitsu's Marc Silvester explains this: "It's about 80 percent freedom, and then sort of 10 percent allowance, and 10 percent you *are* doing it this way. Most general management and educated management styles are weighted the other way around. If you do that, then you are hampering innovation. If you give them a structured career and they follow a structured career, you are going to get a structured outcome and a structured individual. Fantastic for those individuals, but you are never going to change the game. You are never going to bring something special out of people or special to the organization, and you have to take a risk."

Another perspective comes from Nestlé's Jim Singh:

I believe in exposing people to a little of that rain—maybe giving them an umbrella in their hand and then sending them out in the rain. I think we all need discipline, but discipline doesn't necessarily need to be punitive. If discipline has to be punitive, in a team it could be disastrous. But I think discipline in terms of respect for each other, working in terms of a preagreed framework or respecting that you can't just go in and do your own stuff because that may appeal to you. That kind of discipline to always keep shaping and molding the situation, I think everybody needs; sometimes clever people more than others because their egos are a bit bigger, and when you work in a team, you have to suppress your ego.

This set of distinctions led us to another idea. To lead clever people, you need to empathize with them—to have a kind of affinity with them. And remember, clever people like other clever people who are similar to themselves. But they also need discipline. This led us to develop a simple matrix of affinity and discipline (see figure 6-1).

There are several points to be made. First, the most successful organizations in the clever economy exhibit high affinity and clear discipline. Examples include those we have featured at the

FIGURE 6-1

Affinity and discipline matrix

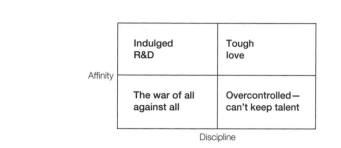

beginning of each part: EA, McLaren, and Cisco. But there are others, like Microsoft. In this quadrant, clever people—and their organizations—thrive. They have fun, and they deliver results.

But there are dangers. Prolonged success can lead organizations to start believing their own propaganda. This always a dangerous sign. The board—you may remember, itself a clever team—has a vital role to play in challenging comfortable assumptions about the organization and the reasons for its success. Good boards combine the roles of enthusiastic advocacy and disciplined critique.

Then there are those with high affinity and low discipline. They are characterized by high sociability—clever people wanting to self-select, hanging out with each other, and choosing work that interests them. In its classically self-critical way, Arup recognizes that it can sometimes face some of these issues. But it also recognizes that great things sometimes happen when the stars are "naturally" aligned. The problem is, it may not happen enough! Indeed, the fashionable way to lead clever people in the 1950s and 1960s was to create an ivory tower. Organizations put up buildings overlooking lakes, oceans, or mountains, populated them with their smartest people, provided money and resources, and retreated 10 yards to await the creative explosion. "In the 1970s, 1980s, and 1990s, my own experience was that 'ivory tower approach' was demonstrated repeatedly to be wrong," reflects Craig Fields.

Highly disciplined organizations with low affinity for clever people aspire to predictable but complex outcomes. For example, the operations and IT functions of global investment banks are harangued daily to deliver on their promises and, by the way, reduce the cost of trade at the same time. Inside these organizations, however, it often doesn't feel that they have the time and space to think creatively. They complain that they are pressured to produce one quick fix after another. This fundamental tension may help explain why so many major IT projects disappoint.

We have noticed one rather alarming trend. As organizations, often under external pressure from the market and the analysts, seek to increase levels of discipline, they create places where clever people don't want to be. They are trying to move from the top left to the bottom right but may kill the empathy yet not achieve the discipline. Here life seems nasty, brutish, and short. Does this explain the flight of clever people from organizations? And could this get worse as a result of the current turbulence?

GENERATE MEANING

Max Weber—in his masterly dissection of power relationships—distinguishes between three types of authority: traditional, charismatic, and rational-legal. Traditional authority typically holds together organizations like kinship groups—it is based upon the belief in the "sanctity of age old rules and powers."[4] Charismatic authority rests upon the peculiar and extraordinary characteristics of particular individuals. Rational legal authority—the dominant form of authority in modern organizations—rests upon the existence of a set of rules and offices with clearly defined and specified jurisdiction.

To these we would add a fourth type: moral authority—a legitimacy that rests upon the communication of a powerful, overarching purpose and is underpinned by a set of shared values held in common by the leader and the led.

Louise Makin puts it very clearly: "Clever people want to work with people they respect, doing meaningful things in a company that's respected externally. The fact that you can contribute to saving a life somewhere is important. We should always have to find some sort of emotional connection."

Jonathan Neale puts it equally clearly for McLaren: "What's great here is that the mission-vision-values isn't that difficult to articulate. It's win, and win is immediately quantifiable, publicly recognizable, and we're tested on that proposition fortnightly from March to October. And when it goes well, it's great and you can go to a dinner party, a school, or a club or go anywhere, without people asking what do you do? I work for McLaren. Oh, that's interesting! When it's going badly, it's also equally true. There is nowhere to hide . . . every schoolboy, milkman, family member, the guy you buy the paper from—anybody—will give you an instant appraisal—'you messed up on Sunday!' And it's a very personal, polarizing, and grounding experience, being publicly tested once a fortnight."

McLaren is a glamorous organization (so, too, in different ways are EA and Cisco), but our view is that many organizations do interesting and valuable things, from banks to retailers, insurers to food suppliers. The task of the clever leader is to find and articulate these clever things.

This concern with meaning relates to a fundamental constituent of organizational cultures: namely their capacity to generate shared value systems. For example, the people at Arup would argue that they require less rule-based discipline as a result of their deeply shared values. Organizations can be coordinated through shared values in the same way as they can by shared rules.

We can see what goes wrong when there is no consensus around values—when the sales force in a pharmaceutical company makes exaggerated claims for a new drug, when a front office in a bank deceives clients, or more dramatically we see it very often in the case of mergers and acquisitions.

In one newly merged pharmaceutical company we observed, an attempt to bring together the best of both cultures that produced the new firm resulted only in confusion and infighting as two organizations with very different values struggled to discover "what they stood for." Searching for cohesion, they found only fragmentation.

The people we have met during this research are as much motivated by the search for meaning as they are by the acquisition of stock options. For clever organizations, the challenge is to become a source of meaning and purpose for the clever people on whom they depend.

KEEP TALKING

The kinds of complex organizations that we have discussed in this book require the sophisticated leadership of interfaces. This is as true for Clever Inc. (Nestlé was our example) as it is for Clever Services (PwC) and Clever Collectives (Google). In essence, the issue is this: clever organizations require structural solutions to the leadership of complexity while knowing that any structural solution rests upon nonstructural competences around collaboration and trust.

In organization design, these are called *lateral integration devices*. They are structural arrangements that bring people together from across the organization in order to tackle complex, multidisciplinary problems. They range from simple solutions— project teams through task forces, liaison posts—right up to the full complexity of the matrix structures commonly found in many knowledge-based organizations. It is hard to imagine, for example, designing an innovative pharmaceutical company that didn't exhibit structural complexity. Indeed, much modern management development has been concerned with giving executives the kind of influencing skills and tolerance of ambiguity that these structures require.

But there is a paradox. None of these structural arrangements can work without the underpinning of widespread trust.[5] There are no structural fixes that are not underpinned by culture.

Clearly, the modern knowledge-based business—whether in high-tech science or professional services—requires collaborative communities in order to bring together diverse competences. These are created through three ingredients: personal relationships, mutual purpose, and trust.[6] The leadership task is to facilitate all of these. Jay Galbraith cites the example of John Gage, the chief scientist at Sun Microsystems, who travels the world stitching together the clever people at Sun. He describes his job as "keeping the smartest people at Sun thinking, talking and working together."[7] Remember, too, how Lucy Gill at Kantar held together her set of complex relationships through travel and face time?

You might ask yourself, what makes these leaders collect the million air miles that it takes to maintain these high-trust networks? Well, curiously, there is a real joy to be had from successfully leading clever people.

REALLY CARE

It sounds trite, perhaps, but the leaders we talked to really cared about those in their charge and the objective of the organization. They were as wrapped up in success as some of their clever people were focused on their projects. We asked McLaren's Jonathan Neale how he feels on a Monday morning if his team has lost a race. "Just humiliated, usually," he said. The color drained slightly from his face. "You feel that we let this notion of what being McLaren is, down." Neale has an omnipresent sense of what the McLaren name and legend means. The team's headquarters is state of the art but is also heavy with the expectations created by history. It exudes meaning. In the trophy cabinet, the helmets of famous drivers are on display: John Watson, Mika Hakkinen, Nigel Mansell, Kimi Raikkonen, David Coulthard. They are a constant reminder of what it all means. It is as much emotional as it is cerebral.

Kamlesh Pande explains what leading clevers means for him:

> They compel me to be intellectually alive. After thirty years of my technical career, I can easily become oblivious as far as technology is concerned. And if I were not working with clever people, I would automatically, without realizing, have fallen into oblivion, and I would be totally out of touch as far as technology and the latest tools and techniques are concerned. So these are the people who compel me to be in touch with what is happening today. And if I am in touch with what is happening today, I have no difficulty in getting in touch with what is going to happen two years hence and four years hence. The second thing is, among the clever people, I would like to be closely associated with youngsters who are clever, because that makes me forget my age. I feel young.

Clear and simple rules, shared meaning, continuous dialogue, and really caring—this sounds like the stuff of a clever HR strategy.

Cleverness is not some sort of elixir of life. But the curiosity that is fundamental to cleverness is the essential lifeblood of the modern organization. Understanding, organizing, leading, and maximizing this is a great challenge. In the clever economy, only the curious will thrive. Any questions?

When you write books like this, you can sometimes create the impression that life in the clever organization is a little hard—populated by difficult and capricious divas, with leaders struggling to create order from a relentless tide of chaos. We certainly do not want to leave you with that impression. As we neared the completion of this book, three of the organizations that we studied experienced the joy of tremendous success.

First, in a pulsating final race, Lewis Hamilton claimed the Formula One World Championship for the McLaren team. It was a magical moment. But it wasn't just Hamilton's overtaking maneuver on the last lap of the last race that secured success. Indeed, millions of Formula One fans around the world held their breath as Hamilton watched another driver with dry tires overtake him in the rain. Hamilton seemed to have forfeited the World Championship, only to roar past the same car just yards before the finish line as it slowed to a crawl, its tires losing their grip on the slick surface. The move was timed to perfection by a team of dedicated and clever race engineers who made canny calculations around the timing of tire changes on a slippery circuit. On the strength of their clever calculations, Hamilton became a deserving world champion. It was a wonderful example of all that we have learned about clever individuals, teams, and organizations.

Second, Arup saw the completion of several stunning projects around the world: at Dubai International Airport (the world's largest single terminal), at Beijing International Airport (a radical sustainable design), and at London Heathrow's Terminal 5 (the largest single-span structure in the United Kingdom). Fresh from its triumphs at the Beijing Olympics, with the "Bird's Nest"–styled Olympic stadium and the magnificent "Water Cube"–inspired aquatics center, it is now turning its attention to ambitious projects for the 2012 London Olympics.

Finally, Electronic Arts' *Spore* saw the light of commercial day for the first time. This took us back to our conversations with the people involved in the project: Will Wright, the originator; his *Spore* colleagues Ocean Quigley and Lucy Bradshaw; the company's original one-man marketing department, Bing Gordon; the executive, David Gardner. EA's *Spore* became one of the most successful and innovative games ever launched, winning industry prizes and the adulation of gamers all over the world. Will Wright's original idea was vindicated, but he stresses that *Spore* was the product of a complex team effort sustained over many years.

Many millions of dollars and countless hours of human labor and imagination have been invested in all of these projects. Yet any one of them could have been a failure. That they were not is a testament not just to the clever people involved but also to their leaders and organizations.

We have a feeling that this is not the most important thing. Success and failure are relative. Success in the clever economy has multiple measures. Commercial success is one, but there is a real sense among the clever people and those who lead them at EA, Google, the NHS in the United Kingdom, and the many other organizations we have encountered, that giving clever people the license, the freedom, the environment, the culture, the necessary discipline to express and develop their talent is success in itself. "The game allows you to create entirely new worlds," promises Will Wright.[8] The challenge in the clever economy is to unleash that potential. We hope we have shown that it can be done.

NOTES

INTRODUCTION

1. There are also similarly curious and paradoxical connections between the work of the American Marxist Harry Braverman and key management theories. Braverman insisted that work in capitalist societies is inevitably deskilled. In his notion of scientific management, Frederick Taylor positively recommended deskilling by separating work into the labor of conception (thinking) and execution (doing). Harry Braverman, *Labor and Monopoly Capital* (New York: Monthly Review Press, 1998).

2. The bureaucratic organization, therefore, expresses rationality without morality. The organizations of the clever economy are much closer to the expression of what Weber calls *value rational action*, which is directed to an overriding ideal.

3. Emile Durkheim, the third member of the triumvirate that set the agenda for modern social theory, was obsessed with the consequences of the division of labor, which he believed characterized the modern era. He believed that the division of labor needed to supply not just efficiency but a shared sense of meaning and moral purpose.

4. Quotations are taken from our research interviews unless otherwise stated. A full list of interviewees can be found in the acknowledgments section.

5. James MacGregor Burns, *Leadership* (New York: Harper & Row, 1978).

6. Warren Bennis and Burt Nanus, *Leaders* (New York: HarperCollins, 1985).

CHAPTER 1

1. See http://www.spore.com/.

2. *PC News* reported that in 2007 the *Sims* games in the top ten PC retail games titles sold more than 1.5 million copies. The American PC games market was worth some $910 million in 2007, and the computer and video games market totaled $18.5 billion. *PC News,* "PC Retail Games Dip in 2007," January 25, 2008.

3. Gary Hamel, "Management 2.0," *Labnotes*, no. 7, February 2008.

4. Jay W. Lorsch and Thomas J. Tierney, *Aligning the Stars* (Boston: Harvard Business School Press, 2002).

5. Bradford C. Johnson, James M. Manyika, and Lareina A. Yee, "The Next Evolution in Interactions," *McKinsey Quarterly*, no. 4 (2005).

6. Interestingly, Humer's observation appears to be confirmed by research. A 2007 study by the consulting firm Booz Allen Hamilton surveyed the world's largest corporate R&D spenders. It found no correlation between how much companies spend on R&D and their innovation success. Booz Allen Hamilton, *Global Innovation 1000* (McLean, VA: Booz Allen Hamilton, December 2007).

7. Gary Hamel, *The Future of Management* (Boston: Harvard Business School Press, 2007).

8. Shawn Tully, "What Were They Smoking," *Fortune,* November 26, 2007.

9. There has been a resurgence of interest in craft work, exemplified by Richard Sennett's *The Craftsman* (London: Allen Lane, 2008).

CHAPTER 2

1. For a recent discussion, see Linda Hill, "Where Will We Find Tomorrow's Leaders?" *Harvard Business Review*, January 2008.

CHAPTER 3

1. This example is drawn with permission from Des Dearlove and Stephen Coomber, *Architects of the Business Revolution* (Milford, CT: Capstone, 2001).

2. R. Meredith Belbin, *Management Teams: Why They Succeed or Fail* (Oxford: Butterworth-Heinemann, 1981).

3. Paul Glen, *Leading Geeks* (San Francisco: Jossey-Bass, 2003), 61–62.

4. Olga Wojtas, "200 Scientists Join Forces," *Times Higher Education Supplement,* January 25, 2008.

5. Glen, *Leading Geeks,* 46, 211.

6. Ibid., 33–34, 37.

7. Sumantra Ghoshal (LVMH case study, unpublished, London Business School).

8. Quoted in Michael Maccoby, "Health Care Organizations as Collaborative Learning Communities," in *The Firm as a Collaborative Community*, eds. Charles Heckscher and Paul S. Adler (Oxford: Oxford University Press, 2006), 262.

CHAPTER 5

1. Daniel H. Pink, *Free-Agent Nation* (New York: Business Plus, 2002).

2. Stephen R. Barley and Gideon Kunda, *Gurus, Hired Guns, and Warm Bodies* (Princeton, NJ: Princeton University Press, 2004), 289–291.

3. Gary Hamel, "Management 2.0," *Labnotes*, no. 7, February 2008.

4. According to Gary Hamel, "Studies show that less than 20 percent of employees around the world are highly engaged in their work. This is a potentially debilitating handicap for organizations competing in today's 'creative economy'. Disengaged employees may be obedient, industrious, and smart, but they are unlikely to bring their initiative, creativity and passion to work—even though, as individuals, they may be richly endowed with these high value capabilities. The right tools, a compelling sense of mission, access to information, the freedom to chose one's work, high caliber colleagues, a stimulating physical environment— these are just a few of the things that help to amplify individual accomplishment." Ibid.

5. Costas Markides and Paul Geroski, "Racing to Be Second," *Business Strategy Review* (Winter 2004); and Constantinos C. Markides and Paul A. Geroski, *Fast Second* (San Francisco: Jossey-Bass, 2004).

6. For a sensitive and detailed insight into the way divisions of labor shift within professional organizations such that the "clever" work of credentialed professional groups is actually undertaken by noncredentialed groups, see Andrew Abbott, *The System of Professions: An Essay on the Division of Expert Labor* (Chicago: University of Chicago Press, 1988). The observation confirms our view that clever work and clever people can routinely be found all over organizations.

CHAPTER 6

1. Des Dearlove, "Ways of Thinking for the 21st Century," *In View*, no. 16 (January 2008).

2. Alvin W. Gouldner, *Patterns of Industrial Bureaucracy* (New York: The Free Press, 1954).

3. From a BBC TV documentary on the Berlin Philharmonic on tour in Asia, 2008.

4. Anthony Giddens, *Capitalism and Modern Social Theory*, vol. 1 (Cambridge: Cambridge University Press, 1973), 156, 226.

5. The argument is close to Emile Durkheim's critique of social contract theorists. Durkheim insists that no form of contract can sufficiently specify rights and obligations and that all contracts rest upon what he calls noncontractual elements of contract.

6. Janine Nahapiet and Sumantra Ghoshal, "Social Capital, Intellectual Capital, and the Organizational Advantage," *Academy of Management Review* 23, no. 2 (1998).

7. Richard Rappaport, "Speaking with the Enemy," *Fast Company,* April 1996.

8. As we completed our book, Will Wright left EA to concentrate on another new world: Stupid Fun Club (given our book's title, what an irony!). Stupid Fun Club is an entertainment think tank in which EA is an investor. Is this the future for clever organizations?

INDEX

ABOUT THE AUTHORS

Rob Goffee and Gareth Jones are Europe's leading experts on organizational culture, leadership, and change. They are past winners of the prestigious McKinsey Award for the best article in *Harvard Business Review,* entitled "Why Should Anyone Be Led by You?" The huge interest it generated led to a five-year journey exploring authentic leadership. Their book of the same title was the culmination of that research and was published by Harvard Business School Press in 2006. In 2008 their article "Leading Clever People" won a second-place McKinsey Award.

Rob Goffee is Professor of Organizational Behavior at London Business School, where he teaches in the world-renowned Senior Executive Program. An internationally respected teacher and facilitator, Rob has taught executives from some of the world's leading companies, including Nestlé, LVMH, Roche, and Arup. He also consults to the boards of a number of FTSE 100 companies.

Gareth Jones is a fellow of the Centre for Management Development at London Business School and a visiting professor at Spain's IE Business School in Madrid. In a career that has uniquely spanned both the academic and the business worlds, Gareth was director of human resources and internal communications at the

British Broadcasting Corporation (BBC); and at Polygram, then the world's largest recorded music company, he was senior vice president for global human resources. Gareth has worked extensively in high-tech companies, in professional services, notably with PwC, in global fast moving consumer goods companies and widely in the creative industries.

Rob and Gareth are the authors of *The Character of a Corporation* (1998) and *Why Should Anyone Be Led by You?* (2006). They are the founding partners of Creative Management Associates, a consultancy focused on organizations where creativity is a source of competitive strength. They can be reached at www.why shouldanyonebeledbyyou.com.